GREAT
SCIEN
TISTS

Immunologists and Virologists

Cavendish
Square

New York

**St. John's School
Lower Library
Houston, TX**

Published in 2014 by Cavendish Square Publishing, LLC
303 Park Avenue South, Suite 1247, New York, NY 10010

Copyright © 2014 by Cavendish Square Publishing, LLC

First Edition

Library of Congress Cataloging-in-Publication Data
Immunologists and virologists / by Ranès C. Chakravorty, et. al.
p. cm. — (Great scientists)
Includes index.
ISBN 978-1-62712-560-4 (hardcover) ISBN 978-1-62712-561-1 (paperback) ISBN 978-1-62712-562-8 (ebook)
1. Immunologists — Biography. 2. Immunology — Juvenile literature. 3. Virologists — Juvenile literature. 4. Viruses — Juvenile literature. I. Title.
QR180.72.S23 C43 2014
616.079—d23

Editorial Director: Dean Miller; Editorial Assistant: Amy Hayes; Art Director: Jeffrey Talbot; Designer: Joseph Macri; Production Manager: Jennifer Ryder-Talbot; Production Editor: Andrew Coddington; Photo Researchers: Laurie Platt Winfrey, Carousel Research, Inc.; Joseph Marci; Amy Greenan; and Julie Alissi, J8 Media

Contents

An Introduction to Great Scientists: *Immunologists and Virologists*

Science offers an ever-expanding and seemingly ever-changing array of facts and theories to explain the workings of life and the universe. Behind its doors, we can explore fascinating worlds ranging from the tiny—the spiral ladder of DNA in every human cell and the particle zoo of quarks and mesons in every atom—to the unimaginably vast—the gradual, often catastrophic shifting of continents over the globe and the immense gravitational fields surrounding black holes in space. Unfortunately, the doors of science often remain shut to students and the general public, who worry they are unable to understand the work done in these technical fields.

Great Scientists seeks to serve as a key. Its goal is to introduce many notable researchers and concepts, sparking interest and providing jumping-off points for gaining further knowledge. To this end, these books offer a select survey of scientists and their accomplishments across disciplines, throughout history, and around the world. The life stories of these individuals and the descriptions of their research and accomplishments will prove both informational and inspirational to budding scientists and to all those with inquisitive minds. For some, learning the paths of these scientists' lives will enable ambitious young students to follow in their footsteps.

Science disciplines are foundational by nature. The work done by the earliest pioneers in a specific field often inspires and informs the next generation of minds, who take the findings and discoveries of their heroes and mentors and further the body of knowledge in a certain area. This progress of scientific inquiry and discovery increases the world's understanding of existing theories and tenants, blazing trails into new directions of study. Perhaps by reading this work, the next great immunologists or virologists will discover their spark of creativity. Whether interested in the theoretical sciences, mathematics, or the applied fields of engineering and invention, students will find these life stories proof that individuals from almost any background can be responsible for key discoveries and paradigm-shifting thoughts and experiments.

The Organization of *Immunologists and Virologists*

This volume profiles thirty-three representative figures in the history of immunology and virology. Entries are generally 800 to 1,700 words in length, with some longer essays covering individuals who made numerous significant contributions to the development of their fields, such as Louis Pasteur, Jonas Salk, Alick Isaacs, Alexander Fleming, Robert Koch, Joseph Lister, and Edward Jenner. In addition to celebrating famous names that made great strides in scientific inquiry and paved the way for others to follow, this book gives credit to individuals and groups who have gone largely unrecognized, such as women and minorities, as well as many contemporary scientists and researchers who are making the newest advances in their field.

The profile of each scientist begins with a list of their areas of achievement, as many of these individuals had impact in more than one discipline. Louis Pasteur made significant contributions in the fields of medicine and chemistry, as well as bacteriology and immunology. Many more like him had such an influence in multiple sciences that inclusion in several different books would be logical, but selections were made to place each scientist in the field most emblematic of their work. After a brief statement of that individual's contribution to science, a timeline covers major life events, including birth and death dates, major awards and honors, and milestones in the scientist's education, research, employment, and private life. The entry then details the struggles and triumphs that characterize the lives of many who pursue knowledge as a career.

The Science Behind the Scientist

An important goal of the Great Scientist series is to expand a reader's understanding of science, not just cover the biographical data of specific scientists. To that end, each profile contains one or more sidebars within the article that provide a simple snapshot introduction to a key topic within the featured scientist's achievements, including theories, research, inventions, or discoveries. While the subjects are not covered

in painstaking detail, there is enough information for readers to gain a working knowledge of topics important to the fields of immunology and virology and their applications.

Illustrating the Science

Several of the sidebars in this book are accompanied by diagrams that help to reinforce the information presented through graphical representation of complex theories and discoveries. In addition, wherever possible, a photograph, painting, or sculpture of the profiled scientist is provided, although there are no likenesses available for some of history's earliest contributors.

Additional Resources

Each profile ends with a two-part bibliography, pointing readers to some of the most significant books and papers written by the particular scientist, as well as other content written about the subject. It is worth noting that these bibliographies are selected works and by no means a complete listing—many of these scientists have contributed dozens of works. The book concludes with a glossary that offers clear definitions of selected terms and concepts, and a comprehensive index that allows readers to locate information about the people, concepts, organizations, and topics covered throughout the book.

Skill Development for Students

Great Scientists: Immunologists and Virologists can serve as a basic biographical text on a specific individual or as a source of enrichment for students looking to know more about an entire scientific field. It is an excellent reference for reading and writing assignments, or it can be a foundational work for major research and term papers. The bibliographies at the end of the profiles and sidebars are invaluable for students looking to learn more about a specific individual or topic.

Aretaeus of Cappadocia

Disciplines: Medicine, pharmacology, physiology, and psychiatry

Contribution: Aretaeus, an important early physician in Greece, described the nature of many diseases, such as diabetes mellitus and tetanus, on the basis of observation and rational interpretation.

probably 2nd century AD	Born in Cappadocia, Roman Empire (now Turkey). Practices medicine, writes many texts on diseases and treatments, and dies, place and date unknown
6th century	First mentioned by such Greco-Roman authors as Aëtius of Amida, Alexander of Tralles, and Paul of Aegina
1552	His works are rediscovered when a Latin translation is published by Junius Paulus Crassus
1554	The first Greek edition of his works is published by Jacobus Goupylus
1856	The first English translation of his works is published by Francis Adams on behalf of the Sydenham Society

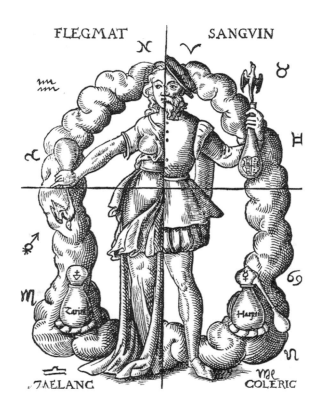

Historical Background

Almost nothing is known about the life of Aretaeus (pronounced "ar-uh-TEE-us") of Cappadocia. His name, at least, indicates that he was born in Cappadocia, Asia Minor, a region of Turkey about 200 miles south of Ankara.

In the centuries immediately before and after the beginning of the Christian era, Asia Minor was colonized and ruled by Greeks. Before that, the area had been under Persian rule from the time of Alexander of Macedon. It became a part of the eastern Roman Empire at the beginning of the Christian era, but the nature of the inhabitants and the culture remained essentially Greek through this time. Many of the most famous Greek physicians were of this Asiatic stock.

A Contemporary of Galen

Indirect evidence suggests that Aretaeus flourished in the 2nd century AD and could have been a contemporary of the celebrated Greek physician

The Description of Diseases

In his description of a disease, Aretaeus depicted the characteristics of the illness with precise observation and little theory.

The great physician Hippocrates depended on observation of the patient and rejected supernatural causes of disease. Aretaeus also used inspection, palpation, and percussion in his clinical examination of patients, and many of his descriptions of diseases are superior to those of Hippocrates.

Greek medicine was based on a theory of the four humors: blood, phlegm, yellow bile, and black bile. With these were interspersed, either in conjunction or separately, qualities such as hot, cold, moist, and dry. Aretaeus was the protagonist of a school that believed in pneuma, a vital force. His concepts of human physiology and anatomy were generally as erroneous as those of his contemporaries.

Thus, Aretaeus believed the heart to be the seat of the soul and animal heat, the source of respiration and life. He thought that it drew in pneuma through the lungs and distributed it throughout the body through the aorta and the arteries. The liver was thought to be the source of veins and to produce blood and bile from food brought to it by the stomach and intestines. The blood was then carried to the heart by the venae cavae.

Aretaeus' description of the kidneys, the urinary bladder, and the brain are largely correct, although he believed (as did his contemporaries) that the brain secreted phlegm. His characterization of the uterus is entirely fanciful: he portrays it as a mobile organ with a capricious tendency.

Aretaeus described many diseases with great clarity. He is probably best known for his description of a wasting disease associated with unquenchable thirst and frequent, massive urination. He called this disease *diabetos* (today known as diabetes mellitus) and noted that death is rapid once the disease is fully established.

He characterized tetanus masterfully. He noted the forward-bending (opisthotonos) and backward-bending (emprosthotonos) forms and recognized the relationship with punctured wounds and abortion in women (although he also mentioned a blow to the neck or severe cold as other possible causes). He described the severe spasm of the jaws that prevents opening of the mouth, the impossibility of a cure, and the quick, fatal course.

He discussed jaundice arising from obstruction of the bile passages going from the gallbladder to the intestines, which causes the gallbladder to dilate, the stool to become like clay, and the skin to turn a yellowish-green. His explanation of jaundice produced by obstruction is correct, but he wrongly believed that it could arise in connection with the spleen, colon, stomach, and kidneys.

Aretaeus recognized the stoppage of urine from bladder stones and recommended diuretics and other measures for relief. He mentioned the use of a catheter and possible operative removal of a bladder stone. He also offered excellent descriptions of lung diseases, epilepsy, and such psychiatric conditions as mania, melancholia, and hysteria.

His therapeutic measures were rational for his time, and he used many herbs and specific foods. However, he also recommended bloodletting, although he warned against excess.

Bibliography

Allbutt, Sir Thomas. *Greek Medicine in Rome.* New York: Macmillan, 1921.

Garrison, Fielding H. *An Introduction to the History of Medicine.* 4th ed. Reprint. Philadelphia, Pa.: W. B. Saunders, 1929.

Henschen, F. "On the Term Diabetes in the Works of Aretaeus and Galen," *Medical History* 13, no. 2 (April, 1969).

Kotsopoulos, S. "Aretaeus the Cappadocian on Mental Illness," *Comprehensive Psychiatry* 27, no. 2 (March/April, 1986).

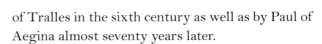

Galen. One eminent authority has stated that Aretaeus was active around the year 50 AD.

Both Galen and Aretaeus were greatly influenced by Hippocratic teaching. They also show similarity in their knowledge of anatomy and in their preferred methods of treatment. They never mention each other in their writings, a curious phenomenon that has been explained as a rivalry.

Clues to His Life

The Roman Empire was in its days of glory at this time, while the Greek Ptolemies ruled over northern Egypt, where Alexandria was a great center of learning, especially for medical and scientific studies. Although Romans held the political power, Greek teaching and practice had become the intellectual driving force. Many Greek physicians came to Rome, however, to establish their practice and seek their fortune.

Aretaeus probably studied in Alexandria, as his writings discuss diseases common in that area. He later practiced or spent some time in Rome, as he mentions Roman foods and wines. The actual place of his practice and the date of his death, though, remain unknown.

Aretaeus wrote in Ionic Greek, a variety of the language that was not in much use at this late date. The Hippocratic Corpus, a collection of sixty medical treastises that probably predated Aretaeus' time by 400-500 years, was written in Ionic Greek, but the language commonly employed during the second century was the more modern Attic Greek. Aretaeus' use of Ionic Greek has been ascribed to his respect for Hippocrates.

Obscurity

After Hippocrates, Aretaeus can be considered the most observant and rational of the Greek medical authors. It is thus surprising that his work was not discussed in any extant texts of the following 300 years. He is finally mentioned by such Greco-Roman authors as Aëtius of Amida and Alexander of Tralles in the sixth century as well as by Paul of Aegina almost seventy years later.

He was also totally neglected by the Arabs, who had great respect for the Greco-Roman medical authors and translated many of their ancient texts into Syriac, and later Arabic and Persian. The resurgence of medical knowledge in Europe started through the introduction of these Arab medical texts and, as the Arabs had ignored Aretaeus, so did the early European medical schools.

Rediscovery

The rediscovery of Aretaeus' opus was quite accidental. With the invention of printing and the rebirth of academic activity, large numbers of ancient Greek and Latin texts were printed. The first edition of the works of Aretaeus was a 1552 Latin translation by Junius Paulus Crassus, a professor in Pavia, Italy, who described the original as "an old and worm-eaten book written in Greek, which accidentally has fallen into my hands."

The first Greek edition of Aretaeus' works was published in 1554 from Paris by Jacobus Goupylus, who brought out a Latin edition the same year and a more complete, revised Latin edition in 1581. A number of Greek-Latin editions were subsequently published in Germany and England.

Evidence of the importance of Aretaeus' place in the Hippocratic tradition is an edition of 1735 under the direction of Herman Boerhaave, who had already edited the texts of Hippocrates and Galen. Boerhaave, the most famous European physician and teacher of his time, was known as *Hippocrates redivivus* ("Hippocrates reborn"). His edition is noted for its excellent comments and detailed indexes.

The first Greek-English edition was published in 1856 by Francis Adams on behalf of the Sydenham Society. Unfortunately, the reprint of this edition by the Classics of Medicine Library in 1990 omits Adams' valuable introduction. In addition, an excellent Greek-German edition edited by Karl Hunde was published in 1923.

Books by Aretaeus on fever, surgery, gynaecology, prophylaxis, and pharmacy have been mentioned in other texts but have never been found.

Bibliography

By Aretaeus

On the Causes and Symptoms of Acute Diseases: Books I and II.

On the Causes and Symptoms of Chronic Diseases: Books I and II.

On the Cure of Chronic Diseases: Book I.

On the Therapeutics of Acute Diseases: Books I and II.

On the Therapeutics of Chronic Diseases: Book II.

These extant works were written in Greek. The English titles are taken from *The Extant Works of Aretaeus, the Cappadocian.* Adams, Francis, ed. and trans. London: Sydenham Society, 1856. Reprint. Birmingham, Ala.: Classics of Medicine Library, 1990.

About Aretaeus

Leopold, E. "Aretaeus the Cappadocian: His Contribution to Diabetes Mellitus," *Annuals of Medical History 2* (1930).

Kudlien, Fridolf. "Aretaeus of Cappadocia," *Dictionary of Scientific Biography.* Charles Coulston Gillespie, ed. Vol. 2. New York: Charles Scribner's Sons, 1970-.

(Ranès C. Chakravorty)

David Baltimore

Disciplines: Cell biology, immunology, and virology

Contribution: Baltimore shared the 1975 Nobel Prize in Physiology or Medicine for his discovery of the reverse transcriptase enzyme.

Mar. 7, 1938	Born in New York
1964	Earns a Ph.D. in biology from Rockefeller University
1965	Research associate in virology at the Salk Institute of Biological Studies
1968	Associate professor of microbiology at the Massachusetts Institute of Technology (MIT)
1972	Promoted to full professor
1974	Elected to the National Academy of Sciences and the American Academy of Arts and Sciences
1975	Awarded the Nobel Prize in Physiology or Medicine
1976	Helps found the Recombinant DNA Advisory Committee at the National Institutes of Health (NIH)
1979-1982	Serves on the NIH Recombinant DNA Advisory Committee
1982-1990	Director of Whitehead Institute
1990-1991	President of Rockefeller University
1994	Named Ivan R. Cottrell Professor of Molecular Biology and Immunology at MIT
1996	Appointed head of the AIDS Vaccine Research Committee
1997- 2006	President of the California Institute of Technology
1999	Awarded the U.S. National Medal of Science

Early Life

David Baltimore received his early education in the public schools of Great Neck, a suburb of New York City. He became interested in biology while still in high school when he attended a summer session at the Jackson Memorial Laboratory. He entered Swarthmore College in biology, but later switched to chemistry, earning a B.A. in 1960. He spent the summer before his senior year at the Cold Spring Harbor Laboratory.

Baltimore entered graduate school in biophysics at the Massachusetts Institute of Technology (MIT), but his decision to work on animal viruses led him to Albert Einstein Medical College, back to Cold Spring Harbor Laboratory, and then to the Rockefeller University, where he received his Ph.D. in biology.

After two stints as a postdoctoral fellow at MIT and Albert Einstein College, Baltimore won his first independent position, as a research associate in virology at the Salk Institute of Biological Sciences. There, he met virologist Alice S. Huang; they married in 1968. That same year, they returned to MIT, where Baltimore became an associate professor of microbiology.

RNA Viruses

During his second summer at Cold Spring Harbor, Baltimore became interested in viruses that use ribonucleic acid (RNA) instead of deoxyribonucleic acid (DNA) as their genetic material. He wondered, "How does a virus hijack the chemical machinery of a cell and use it to make more virus particles?" One of his answers won for him the 1975 Nobel Prize in Physiology or Medicine, which he shared with Howard Temin and Renato Dulbecco.

Baltimore discovered that vesicular stomatitis virus particles contain an enzyme that copies viral RNA once the virus finds itself inside a cell, and he sought a similar enzyme in retroviruses, which were known to cause cancer in animals. This suggested to Temin in 1964 that these tumor viruses insert their genetic code into that cell's DNA, which required a DNA copy from the viral RNA. This "provirus" hypothesis contradicted the central dogma of molecular genetics and was not well received.

Baltimore had known Temin since they met when the former was a high-school student at Jackson Laboratory. Thinking that his old friend might be right, Baltimore searched for an enzyme that transcribed RNA into DNA—and found it.

Temin performed a similar search, and, when the two friends realized they had made the same discovery independently, they decided to publish their results simultaneously. The enzyme that they discovered was later dubbed "reverse transcriptase."

A Cautious Scientist and Public Servant

Baltimore continued to study retroviruses, including the human immunodeficiency virus (HIV) that

Reverse Transcriptase

Baltimore showed that an enzyme in retroviruses can transcribe ribonucleic acid (RNA) into deoxyribonucleic acid (DNA).

The genetic material that makes up a cell's chromosomes is DNA, which determines the cell's proteins. Many of these proteins are enzymes, which control the chemical reactions in the cell.

A virus is a simple inert organism that invades a living cell and exploits the cell's metabolism to reproduce itself. The infected cell may die, live normally, or become "transformed." A virus, unlike a cell, may have either DNA or RNA as its genetic material.

Before Baltimore's studies, it was known that some RNA-containing viruses cause cancer in animals. Since cancer is uncontrolled cell reproduction, these viruses transform not only the infected cell but all of its descendants. How could a virus containing only RNA become part of the cell's DNA inheritance? It can do so if the viral RNA is transcribed into DNA and combined with the cell's DNA as a "provirus." Baltimore discovered the enzyme, reverse transcriptase, that performs this transcription.

Viruses that use reverse transcription are called retroviruses. This class of viruses includes the human immunodeficiency virus (HIV), which causes acquired immunodeficiency syndrome (AIDS). It is now recognized that reverse transcription occurs in normal cells and is the mechanism behind transposable genetic elements, or "jumping genes."

Reverse transcriptase has become an important reagent used in molecular biology and recombinant DNA techniques.

Bibliography

Temin, Howard M. "RNA-Directed DNA Synthesis," *Scientific American* (January, 1972).

Varmus, Harold. "Reverse Transcription," *Scientific American* (September, 1987).

Stryer, Lubert. *Molecular Design of Life.* New York: W. H. Freeman, 1989.

Skalka, Anna Marie and Stephen P. Goff, eds. *Reverse Transcriptase.* Plainview, N.Y.: Cold Spring Harbor Laboratory Press, 1993.

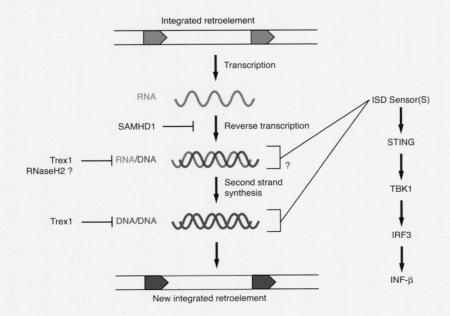

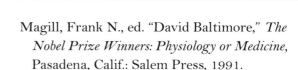
causes acquired immunodeficiency syndrome (AIDS). His research branched out into immunology.

When scientists developed techniques to cut strands of DNA from one organism and splice them into another, some feared that this might be dangerous. In 1974 Baltimore and ten like-minded members of the National Academy of Sciences called for a moratorium on experiments using this "recombinant DNA" technique. The moratorium lasted nearly two years while safety procedures were worked out.

Baltimore was instrumental in founding the Recombinant DNA Advisory Committee at the National Institutes of Health (NIH), to set further rules governing these genetic engineering experiments, and was a member of the committee from 1979 to 1982. He served as one of the chairs of the Committee on a National Strategy for AIDS in 1986. In December 1996 Baltimore was appointed by NIH director Harold Varmus to direct the effort to find an AIDS vaccine.

The following year, he was named president of the California Institute of Technology (Caltech). He continued this role until 2007, when he retired from leadership to pursue research.

Bibliography

By Baltimore

"RNA-Dependent DNA Polymerase in Virions of RNA Tumour Viruses," *Nature*, 1970.

Animal Virology, 1976 (ed., with Alice S. Huang and C. Fred Fox).

Molecular Cell Biology, 1986 (with Harvey Lodish and James Darnell).

About Baltimore

Wasson, Tyler, ed. *Nobel Prize Winners: An H. W. Wilson Biographical Dictionary.* New York: H. W. Wilson, 1987.

Fox, Daniel M., Marcia Meldrum, and Ira Rezak, eds. *Nobel Laureates in Medicine or Physiology: A Biographical Dictionary.* New York: Garland, 1990.

Magill, Frank N., ed. "David Baltimore," *The Nobel Prize Winners: Physiology or Medicine*, Pasadena, Calif.: Salem Press, 1991.

"Caltech president David Baltimore named winner of the 1999 National Medal of Science," http://www.caltech.edu/content/caltech-president-david-baltimore-named-winner-1999-national-medal-science

"David Baltimore," *Encyclopædia Britannica* online, http://www.britannica.com/EBchecked/topic/51022/David-Baltimore

"Division of Biology and Biological Engineering—David Baltimore," California Institute of Technology, http://www.bbe.caltech.edu/content/david-baltimore

(Randy Hudson)

Emil Adolf von Behring

Disciplines: Bacteriology, immunology, and medicine

Contribution: Behring's development of antitoxins to combat diphtheria and tetanus helped eliminate the threat of two dread diseases and opened the way for the medical application of immunology.

Mar. 15, 1854	Born in Hansdorf, Prussia
1866	Enters the gymnasium at Hohenstein, East Prussia
1874	Enters army medical school, the Friedrich-Wilhelm Institute, in Berlin
1878	Graduated and is posted to Royal Charite Hospital in Berlin
1887	Assigned to the Pharmacology Institute, the University of Bonn
1889	Joins Robert Koch at the University of Berlin
1891	Moves to Koch's Institute for Infectious Disease
1891	His antitoxin successfully treats a child with diphtheria
1894	Results of his antitoxin trials are presented at the International Congress of Hygiene, Budapest
1894	Professor of hygiene at the University of Halle
1895	Chair of the Department of Hygiene at University of Marburg
1901	Awarded the First Nobel Prize in Physiology or Medicine
1913	Announces a preventive serum for diphtheria
Mar. 31, 1917	Dies in Marburg, Germany

Early Life

Emil Adolf von Behring (pronounced "BAY-rihng") was born in 1854 in Hansdorf, Prussia, one of thirteen children of August Behring, a local schoolteacher. Emil proved an outstanding student, quickly surpassing his father's ability to serve as his teacher. A local pastor continued his education until Behring entered the gymnasium at Hohenstein in 1866.

Upon his graduation, Behring wished to study medicine, but his options were limited. He initially decided on a career in the ministry, but a friend recommended Behring to the army medical school in Berlin. In 1874 Behring entered the Friedrich-Wilhelm Institute.

Behring's training was rigorous, but the medical corps was noted for its enlightened training by a brilliant faculty. The curriculum included numerous laboratory courses as well as training in languages and the humanities. Behring graduated in 1878, completing a doctoral thesis on eye disease.

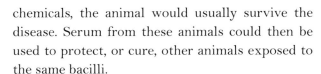

Army Duty and Early Research

Following two years of internship, Behring began his formal military duties. Unmarried, he enjoyed his life as a young officer, once even changing posts because of gambling debts.

Behring also began developing an interest in medical research. He conducted his first formal experiments when assigned to the province of Posen, testing the effectiveness of iodoform (tri-iodomethane) for treatment of wounds. He also enrolled in a course on bacteriological techniques, taught by an associate of Robert Koch.

In 1886 Behring was assigned by the Army Medical Corps to the University of Bonn. It was there that he began his work on bacteriocidal agents, using anthrax as an experimental model. Behring was aware of the extensive work carried out by Koch in the area of germ theory; it was Koch who firmly demonstrated the role of the anthrax bacillus as the etiological agent of the disease. Behring requested an assignment with Koch and, in 1889, joined his laboratory at the University of Berlin.

A Diphtheria Antitoxin

Behring had previously demonstrated that chemical treatment of bacterial wounds could neutralize certain toxins. As a member of Koch's laboratory, he decided to continue this line of research. He was joined in this quest by Shibasaburo Kitasato, the Japanese scientist who had already isolated the agent for tetanus. Moving with Koch to the newly established Institute for Infectious Disease in 1891, Behring and Kitasato began their work on the treatment of both tetanus and diphtheria. It had already been established that both diseases are caused by toxins secreted by their respective etiological agents. Behring reasoned that if the body could survive exposure to these toxins, a lifelong immunity could be established.

Behring and Kitasato found that when rabbits or guinea pigs had been infected with the bacilli, and the site was then treated with certain toxic chemicals, the animal would usually survive the disease. Serum from these animals could then be used to protect, or cure, other animals exposed to the same bacilli.

On December 25, 1891, Behring successfully carried out the first treatment of a child with diphtheria, using serum obtained from a previously immunized animal. Large-scale trials proved equally successful.

International Acclaim

Unfortunately, Behring and Koch soon developed an animosity that quickly escalated into a feud. In 1894 Behring requested a position in a university and was appointed acting Professor of Hygiene at the University of Halle.

Behring found teaching difficult and, requesting another change, was appointed Chair of the Department of Hygiene at the University of Marburg in 1895. That same year, he was also admitted to the nobility, as Emil von Behring. Further honors raised him to the position of *Exzellenz* (excellency) von Behring.

In 1901 Behring was awarded the first Nobel Prize in Physiology or Medicine for his work developing serum therapy. He was honored even by the hereditary enemies of his country, receiving the French Legion of Honor.

Later Years

Despite international acclaim, Behring's last years were often spent in controversy. Like Koch, with whom he continued his feud, he was bogged down in the problem of tuberculosis. Convinced that this disease was caused by a toxin, Behring continued his attempts to develop a therapeutic agent. By 1912 he finally gave up.

Despite poor health, Behring continued his success in the treatment of diphtheria. In 1913 he reported the development of a mixture of diphtheria toxin and antitoxin that proved particularly useful in immunization against the disease.

The Development of a Diphtheria Antitoxin

Behring's development of an antitoxin against diphtheria provided a means to protect or cure children stricken with an often-fatal disease.

In the late nineteenth century diphtheria was among the most dreaded of childhood diseases. In Germany alone, some 100,000 children were afflicted each year, with a mortality rate of approximately 50 percent. Equivalent numbers could be found in other countries. From 1883 until well into the twentieth century, more than half of all deaths among children were the result of this disease.

In 1884 Robert Koch's associate Friedrich Löffler isolated the diphtheria bacillus; in 1889 Émile Roux and Alexandre Yersin demonstrated that the disease results from a toxin produced by the bacillus.

Having recently joined Koch's laboratory, Behring became interested in humoral (soluble) mechanisms by which the body responds to disease. He noted that therapeutic chemicals such as iodine trichloride or sodium chloroaurate, when applied directly to the sites on rabbits that had been infected with either diphtheria or tetanus bacilli, prevented the diseases from developing. The blood from these animals would then neutralize the toxins, rendering them harmless.

Behring continued to test various blood components to determine which fraction provided the best immunity. He found that while whole blood provided some immunity, the liquid portion present after the blood clotted, called serum, contained the highest level of protective power.

Behring and Shibasaburo Kitasato then tested whether the transfer of this immune serum to susceptible rabbits could also protect these animals. The tests were successful, and Behring concluded that a humoral agent in the blood of immunized animals could neutralize the toxin; the agent could also be passively transferred to other animals, thereby providing them with protection. The sooner the serum was provided after infection, the greater was its protective ability. Behring and Kitasato introduced the term "antitoxic" to characterize the substance.

Once Behring worked out the procedures that provided serum with the greatest potency, he decided to test the therapy in humans. At first, he was hesitant, because he was unsure whether large quantities of animal serum could be injected into children safely. Fortunately, Behring found that the necessary quantities were smaller than initially thought. He began the trials in 1892, using serum from immunized animals to treat children at the Charite Hospital who were seriously ill with diphtheria. Among eleven children treated with the serum, nine survived. This contrasted with a death rate of 65 percent among children at the hospital who were not previously treated.

Similar treatment proved equally successful among hundreds of children treated over the next two years. Indeed, in later trials carried out in London, the death rate from diphtheria between 1895 and 1910 dropped from 62 to 10 percent.

The results of Behring's trials, and similar ones carried out by Roux in France, were presented at the International Congress of Hygiene, which was held in Budapest in 1894. Behring's discovery brought him international fame.

Bibliography

De Kruif, Paul. *Microbe Hunters.* New York: Harcourt, Brace & World, 1953.

Lechevalier, Hubert and Morris Solotorovsky *Three Centuries of Microbiology.* New York: Dover, 1974.

Silverstein, Arthur. *A History of Immunology.* San Diego, Calif.: Academic Press, 1989.

In 1914 Behring suffered a broken femur that never properly healed. A severe abscess compounded the problem. Bedridden, he developed pneumonia and died on March 31, 1917.

Bibliography

By Behring

"Über Iodoform und Iodoformwirkung" (iodoform and the use of iodoform), *Deutsche medizinische Wochenschrift*, 1882.

"Über das Zustandekommen der Diphtherie-Immunität und der Tetanus-Immunität bei Thieren" (mechanism of immunity to diphtheria and tetanus in animals), *Deutsche medizinische Wochenschrift*, 1890 (with S. Kitasato).

"Untersuchungen über das Zustandekommen der Diphtherie-Immunität bei Thieren" (studies on the mechanism of immunity to diphtheria in animals), *Deutsche medizinische Wochenschrift*, 1890.

Die Geschichte der Diphtherie: Mit besonderer ber ucksichtigung der Immunit Atslehre, 1893.

Allgemeine Therapie der Infectionskrankheiten, 1899.

The Suppression of Tuberculosis, 1904 (Charles Bolduan, ed.).

"Über ein neues Diphtherieschutzmittel" (a new method for diphtheria treatment), *Deutsche medizinische Wochenschrift*, 1913.

E. v. Behring's Gesammelte Abhandlungen, 1915.

About Behring

Magill, Frank N., ed. "Emil Adolf von Behring," *The Nobel Prize Winners: Physiology or Medicine*, Pasadena, Calif.: Salem Press, 1991.

(Richard Adler)

Jules Bordet

Disciplines: Bacteriology, immunology, and medicine

Contribution: Bordet's Nobel Prize-winning research into the basis of humoral immunity helped lay the groundwork for the science of immunology.

June 13, 1870	Born in Soignies, Belgium
1886-1892	Studies medicine at the University of Brussels
1892	Publishes his first scientific paper
1894-1900	Works at the Pasteur Institute in Paris
1901-1940	Director of the Pasteur Institute in Brussels
1906	Isolates the bacterium responsible for whooping cough
1907-1935	Professor of bacteriology at the University of Brussels
1909	Describes the germ involved in bovine pleuropneumonia
1916	Made a Foreign Member of the Royal Society of London
1920	Awarded the Nobel Prize in Physiology and Medicine
1920	Publishes *Traité de l'immunité dans les maladies infectieuses* (treatise on immunity in infectious diseases)
1930	Elected president of the First International Congress of Microbiology
1933	Serves as president of the scientific council for the Pasteur Institute, Paris
Apr. 6, 1961	Dies in Brussels, Belgium

Early Life

Jules-Jean-Baptiste-Vincent Bordet (pronounced "bawr-DAY") was born in Belgium in 1870 as the son of a schoolteacher. After demonstrating an early interest in chemistry, he enrolled in the University of Brussels at the age of sixteen and graduated as a doctor of medicine in 1892.

During medical school, Bordet carried out experiments in bacteriology, and in 1894 he won a government scholarship to pursue further research. He traveled to Paris to begin studies with Élie Metchnikoff, one of the foremost scientists working in the new fields of bacteriology and immunology.

Immunological Studies in Paris

During his six years in Paris at the Pasteur Institute, Bordet made most of his fundamental discoveries in immunology. He showed that bacteria can be killed by serum (cell-free blood) and that this activity is controlled by two kinds of substances: a heat-sensitive component that Bordet named "alexin" (later called complement) and a heat-resistant component that he named "sensibilizer" (later called antibody).

In several subsequent papers, Bordet elucidated many of the essential characteristics of this phenomenon, and he demonstrated its applicability in a range of experimental situations. His immunological experiments awarded him quite a scientific reputation, and, in 1901, the Belgian government invited him to return to Brussels as director of a research institute.

Back to Brussels

Bordet continued his immunological work in Brussels at the new Pasteur Institute there. He developed the complement fixation test, one of the most widely applicable blood tests in diagnostic microbiology. By 1909 his work was recognized to be of such importance that an English edition of many of his scientific papers, most originally written in French, was published.

Bordet was also active in bacteriology, and in 1906 he isolated the bacterium responsible for whooping cough (*Bordetella pertussis*) from his son, who was sick with the disease. Bordet was particularly gifted at designing media on which fastidious bacteria would grow, and he was the first to cultivate the organism responsible for bovine pleuropneumonia (*Mycoplasma mycoides*) on solid medium. In 1907 he was appointed professor of bacteriology at the University of Brussels.

A Statesman for Science

Bordet continued to perform original scientific studies after World War I, including work on the newly discovered bacteriophage. His direct involvement in research was diminished, however, by his heavy administrative and professional responsibilities. He held both the chair of bacteriology and the directorship of the Pasteur Institute in Brussels. In 1933 Bordet assumed the

The Complement System

The complement system is an important part of the body's defense against infection.

The complement system consists of more than thirty proteins found in the fluid part of the blood, called serum. This system, either on its own or in cooperation with antibodies also found in blood serum, functions to protect the body against infection. Because antibodies and the complement proteins are found in the serum, they are part of the humoral (or noncellular) immune response. The name of the system derives from the fact that it "complements" antibodies, which are the most important part of the humoral immune response.

Because the body is not always engaged in fighting infections, the complement system is normally inactive. It can be activated by several mechanisms, including the presence of an antigen-antibody complex, such as an antibody bound to a bacterial cell (an antigen). Activated complement is associated with several important immune functions, particularly phagocytosis and immune lysis.

In phagocytosis, white blood cells (or phagocytes) neutralize microorganisms such as bacteria and viruses by ingesting and destroying them. Phagocytes only ingest those microorganisms that they recognize as a threat to the body. In order to assist phagocytes in this recognition process, the body "labels" micro-organisms with specific substances; the principal "labels" are antibodies. Once an antibody binds to a bacterial cell, phagocytes readily ingest it. When complement components bind to an antibody-cell complex, the process of phagocytosis is further enhanced. This process of enhancing phagocytosis is called opsonization; complement thus functions as an opsonin.

In immune lysis, activated complement proteins attach themselves to the bacteria-antibody complex and trigger what is termed the complement cascade. The terminal components of this cascade form the membrane attack complex (MAC), which causes the bacterial cell to break open (or lyse). In addition to enhancing phagocytosis and cell lysis, complement is also one of the substances that can initiate inflammation, and it may assist in the development of the immune response.

Bordet was the first person to show that blood contains the two components later identified as antibodies and complement. Although he did not realize that complement is not a single substance but is instead a group of proteins, his contemporaries immediately recognized the importance of his work, which laid the foundation for further studies of this component of the humoral immune system.

Bordet himself understood the practical implications of his discovery of complement, and he made it the foundation of the complement fixation test (CFT). This test was used by August Wassermann in 1906 to detect syphilis, thus making it the first blood test for an infectious disease. The CFT was subsequently applied in the diagnosis of a variety of infectious diseases.

Bibliography

Mayer, Manfred M. "The Complement System," *Scientific American* 229 (November, 1973).

Law, S. K. A. and K. B. M. Reid. *Complement.* 2d ed. Oxford, England: Oxford University Press, 1995.

Roitt, Ivan, Jonathan Brostoff, and David Male. *Immunology.* London: C. V. Mosby, 1996.

prestigious presidency of the scientific council of the Pasteur Institute in Paris, a post that he held until the outbreak of World War II. He also wrote several scientific textbooks at this time, as well as other popular scientific works.

Contemporary recognition of Bordet's scientific work followed quickly on the heels of his stay in Paris. He received numerous scientific awards and distinctions and was made a member of many academies, including the Royal Society of London and the National Academy of Sciences in the United States. In 1920 Bordet received the Nobel Prize in Physiology or Medicine for his work in immunology. He died in 1961 at the age of ninety.

Bibliography

By Bordet
La vie et l'oeuvre de Pasteur, 1902.
Studies in Immunity, 1909.
Traite de l'immunité dans les maladies infectieuses, 1920.
Brèves considérations sur le mode de gouvernement, la liberté, et l'éducation morale, 1945.
Injection et immunité, 1947.
Éléments d'astronomie, destinés aux visiteurs du Planétarium, 1955.

About Bordet
De Kruif, Paul. *Men Against Death*. New York: Harcourt, Brace, 1932.
Beumer, J. "Jules Bordet, 1870–1961," *Journal of General Microbiology* 29 (1962).

(James G. Hanley)

Sir Frank Macfarlane Burnet

Disciplines: Bacteriology, genetics, immunology, and virology

Contribution: Burnet, an accomplished virologist and theoretical immunologist, was best known for his work on the influenza virus, and for his theories on acquired immunological tolerance and clonal selection of antibody formation.

Sept. 3, 1899	Born in Traralgon, Victoria, Australia
1924	Earns an M.D. from the University of Melbourne
1928	Earns a Ph.D. from the University of London
1928-1931	Bacteriologist at the Walter and Eliza Hall Institute
1932-1933	Virologist at the National Institute of Medical Research in London
1934-1965	Assistant director and then director of the Walter and Eliza Hall Institute
1949	Proposes the theory of acquired immunological tolerance
1951	Knighted
1957	Proposes the clonal selection theory of antibody production
1960	Awarded the Nobel Prize in Physiology or Medicine
1961	Named "Australian of the Year"
1965-1978	Serves as president of the Australian Academy of Science
Aug. 31, 1985	Dies in Melbourne, Victoria, Australia

where he studied bacteriophages (viruses that infect bacteria). Based on his work at the Lister Institute, he was granted a Ph.D. degree from the University of London in 1928.

He then worked for several years as a bacteriologist at the Walter and Eliza Hall Institute in Melbourne, Australia, where he continued his work on bacteriophages and made many significant contributions to this field. In particular, he devised a classification system for bacteriophages and elucidated mechanisms by which these viruses replicate within bacterial cells.

In 1932 Burnet accepted a position at the National Institute of Medical Research in London, and his research interests changed from bacterial viruses to animal viruses, a topic that would dominate his scientific career for the next twenty-five years.

Animal Virology

Burnet returned to Australia in 1934 and worked at the Walter and Eliza Hall Institute until 1965, first in the position of assistant director in charge of the virus section and then as director.

After being named director, Burnet decided that all the research programs at the institute should be focused on animal virology, and, in time, the Walter and Eliza Hall Institute became a world-renowned center for virology research, attracting eminent scientists from Europe and America. Gaining the respect of the scientific community abroad was very important to Burnet, as he was fiercely patriotic. He had previously turned down positions at such prestigious locations as Harvard University in order to develop a world-class facility in Australia.

Burnet studied and published papers on a variety of viral diseases such as polio, Q fever, herpes simplex, psittacosis, and influenza. Among his numerous accomplishments were identification of the causative agent of Q fever and development of a method, using chicken embryos, for growing and enumerating viruses. He showed that more

Early Life

Frank Macfarlane Burnet was born in 1899 in the town of Traralgon, in eastern Victoria, Australia. He lived there with his parents and six brothers and sisters until the age of ten, when his family moved to Terang in western Victoria.

As a child, Burnet was interested in nature and loved to spend time outdoors hiking and camping. He participated in Boy Scouts and developed a life-long passion for collecting and studying beetles.

Burnet majored in biology and medicine at Geelong College in Victoria and then continued his education at Ormond College of the University of Melbourne, where he obtained a B.S. in 1922 and an M.D. in 1924.

Early Scientific Career

Burnet completed a medical residency in pathology at the Royal Melbourne Hospital and, in 1926, received a Beit Research Fellowship to the Lister Institute of Preventative Medicine in London,

The Clonal Selection Theory of Antibody Production

Every animal has a diverse array of lymphocytes, each with cell surface receptors specific for one antigen. When an antigen enters the body, it binds to the appropriate lymphocyte and triggers a clonal expansion of the selected lymphocyte.

Lymphocytes are cells that defend the body against harmful foreign substances (antigens), such as disease-causing microorganisms or toxins. B lymphocytes synthesize chemicals called antibodies that bind to and promote the destruction, neutralization, or elimination of antigens.

Any given antibody is specific for only one antigen, meaning that it will bind only to the antigen that stimulated its production. The immune system is capable of producing antibodies against virtually any foreign antigen that may be introduced into the body, even artificial substances that an individual would not normally encounter. With so many possibilities, how does the immune system know which antibody to produce in response to a given antigen?

Prior to 1955, scientists believed that antibody molecules were produced as generic proteins, all with the same structure initially but capable of being modified to react specifically with an antigen. Upon exposure to an antigen, the antibody would fold around the antigen to assume its final chemical structure. This theory, proposed by Linus Pauling in 1940, was known as the instructive or template theory.

In 1955 Niels K. Jerne postulated a selective theory of antibody production, which stated that every animal has a preexisting bank of circulating antibodies, each capable of binding to a different antigen. When an antigen enters the body, it binds to (selects) the appropriate antibody, which then signals lymphocytes to produce large quantities of antibodies with the same structural specificity. Then, in 1957, David Talmadge suggested that the antigen must also somehow trigger the multiplication of the cells responsible for making the matching antibody.

Burnet's clonal selection theory united the concepts of Jerne and Talmadge. According to Burnet, each individual possesses a diverse array of lymphocytes, each capable of producing a specific type of antibody and each carrying, on its cell surface, receptors with the same antigen specificity as the antibody that they are destined to produce. The antigen "selects" a lymphocyte bearing the appropriate receptor and binds to this receptor in a lock-and-key type of interaction. This stimulates the lymphocyte to proliferate (divide many times) and give rise to a large population of genetically identical daughter cells (clones), all of which synthesize and release antibodies specific for the original antigen.

The clonal selection theory is now universally accepted as an explanation of not only B lymphocyte but also T lymphocyte function. T lymphocytes also exhibit antigen specificity and clonal expansion, but, instead of producing antibodies, they destroy infected cells or tumor cells through direct, cell-to-cell contact.

Bibliography

Ada, Gordon L. and Sir Gustav Nossal. "The Clonal Selection Theory," *Scientific American* 257 (August, 1987).

Roitt, Ivan. *Essential Immunology.* London: Blackwell Scientific Publications, 1991.

Benjamini, Eli and Sidney Leskowitz. *Immunology: A Short Course.* New York: Wiley-Liss, 1991.

than one strain of polio virus exists and that new strains of influenza virus arise through genetic mutation. He also pioneered efforts to develop effective vaccines against the more potent strains of influenza.

Immunology

In 1957 Burnet's research interests changed again, this time to immunology (the study of the immune system). As an immunologist, his contributions were more theoretical than experimental, although he maintained an active research program.

Burnet had long been interested in understanding how the immune system defends against infectious or toxic agents (antigens) and, in particular, how it distinguishes between normal body components ("self") and potentially harmful foreign substances ("nonself"). Based on a variety of experimental observations, he proposed the concept of acquired immunological tolerance as an explanation of self-versus-nonself immunological recognition. He shared the 1960 Nobel Prize in Physiology or Medicine with Sir Peter Medawar for this theory.

He also proposed the clonal selection theory of antibody production, which he considered to be the most important accomplishment of his scientific career. This theory provides an explanation for the ability of the immune system to recognize and react against a limitless array of foreign antigens.

Retirement

In 1965 Burnet left the Walter and Eliza Hall Institute and retired from active research. He continued to write books and papers, ranging in scope from highly technical reviews of his research in virology and immunology to nontechnical books on cancer, aging, and human biology. He also served as president of the Australian Academy of Sciences until 1978. He died of cancer at the age of eighty-five in Melbourne, Australia.

Bibliography

By Burnet

Biological Aspects of Infectious Disease, 1940 (also as *The Natural History of Infectious Disease*, 1953).

The Production of Antibodies: A Review and Theoretical Discussion, 1941 (with M. Freeman, A. V. Jackson, and D. Lush).

Influenza: A Survey of the Last Fifty Years in the Light of Modern Work on the Virus of Epidemic Influenza, 1942.

Virus as Organism: Evolutionary and Ecological Aspects of Some Human Virus Diseases, 1945.

The Background of Infectious Diseases in Man, 1946.

Viruses and Man, 1953.

Principles of Animal Virology, 1955.

Enzyme, Antigen, and Virus: A Study of Macro-molecular Pattern in Action, 1956.

The Clonal Selection Theory of Acquired Immunity, 1959.

The Integrity of the Body: A Discussion of Modern Immunological Ideas, 1962.

Autoimmune Diseases: Pathogenesis, Chemistry, and Therapy, 1963 (with I. R. MacKay).

Ciba Foundation Symposium: The Thymus, Experimental and Clinical Studies, 1965.

Biology and the Appreciation of Life, 1966.

Changing Patterns: An Atypical Autobiography, 1968.

Immunological Surveillance, 1969.

Self and Not-Self 1969.

Dominant Mammal: The Biology of Human Destiny, 1970.

Genes, Dreams, and Realities, 1971.

Walter and Eliza Hall Institute, 1915-1965, 1971.

Auto-immunity and Auto-immune Disease: A Survey for Physician or Biologist, 1972.

Intrinsic Mutagenesis: A Genetic Approach to Ageing, 1974.

Biology of Ageing, 1974.

Immunology, 1976.

Immunology, Aging, and Cancer: Medical Aspects of Mutation and Selection, 1976.

Uranium: For Good or Evil?, 1976.
Endurance of Life: The Implications of Genetics for Human Life, 1978.
Credo and Comment: A Scientist Reflects, 1979.
Biological Foundations and Human Nature, 1983.

About Burnet

Magill, Frank N., ed. *The Nobel Prize Winners: Physiology or Medicine*. Pasadena, Calif.: Salem Press, 1991.

Sexton, Christopher. *The Seeds of Time: The Life of Sir Macfarlane Burnet*. Oxford, England: Oxford University Press, 1991.

(Darbie L. Maccubbin)

Max Delbrück

Disciplines: Bacteriology, genetics, and virology

Contribution: Delbrück was responsible for transforming the study of bacterial genetics into an exact science. Along with Salvador Edward Luria and Alfred Day Hershey, he was awarded the 1969 Nobel Prize in Physiology or Medicine for discoveries concerning the replication and genetic structure of viruses.

Sept. 4, 1906	Born in Grunewald, Berlin, Germany
1924-1928	Studies astronomy at the universities of Tübingen and Göttingen
1930	Earns a Ph.D. in theoretical physics from Göttingen
1931	Studies under Niels Bohr on a Rockefeller Foundation fellowship
1935	Publishes "On the Nature of the Gene Mutation and the Gene Structure"
1937	Studies at the California Institute of Technology (Caltech)
1940-1947	Teaches physics at Vanderbilt University in Nashville, Tennessee
1947-1977	Teaches at Caltech
1949	Elected to the National Academy of Sciences
1964	Wins the Kimber Genetics Award
1969	Awarded the Louisa Gross Horowitz Prize of Columbia University
1969	Awarded the Nobel Prize in Physiology or Medicine
Mar. 9, 1981	Dies in Pasadena, California

Early Life

Max Ludwig Henning Delbrück, the youngest of the seven children of Hans and Lina Delbrück, was born on September 4, 1906, in Grunewald, a suburb of Berlin, Germany. Delbrück grew up surrounded by great thinkers. His father was a history professor at the University of Berlin and editor of *Prussian Yearbook*, a political magazine. Famous theologians Adolf von Harnack and Deitrich Bonhoeffer were family friends. Sunday afternoon get-togethers sparked great philosophical and political discussions in which the youngest Delbrück participated.

Delbrück resented his well-known family name and strove to stand out for his own accomplishments. In high school, he developed an interest in astronomy, a field not known well by the other Delbrücks. After his graduation in 1924, he pursued his interest in the stars by studying astronomy at the University of Tübingen and later at the University of Göttingen.

He began writing a dissertation on celestial novas—new stars that suddenly increase in size and become extremely bright. Unfortunately, he did not complete the dissertation because he could not read the English research papers necessary to understand the astrophysics behind these events.

Theoretical Physics

While Delbrück was a student there, Göttingen became a center for studying theoretical physics. He turned his attention from astronomy to quantum mechanics, the newest branch of physics. Quantum mechanics explains the components of atoms and how they absorb light. Delbrück worked out mathematical explanations for the chemical bonding of the element lithium, and, in 1930, he earned his Ph.D. in physics.

In 1931 Delbrück received a Rockefeller Foundation fellowship to continue studying theoretical physics, which allowed him to work with Niels Bohr in Copenhagen. While there, he developed a lifelong friendship with Bohr, who sparked his interest in biology. Bohr and Delbrück were especially interested in the relationship between physics and life, and wondered how the phenomena of existence could occur.

The Delbrück Model

Delbrück returned to Berlin in 1932 to study the uranium atom with Lise Meitner. Over the next five years, the young physicist's interest in biology and genetics grew. He held informal meetings with physicists from the Kaiser-Wilhelm Institute for Biology in Berlin. During these meetings, the participants discussed how quantum mechanics could be used to explain genetic changes called mutations.

In a paper published in 1935, Delbrück and his colleagues theorized that genetic mutations were caused by absorption of packets of radiation, called quanta. Erwin Schrödinger, a famous Austrian physicist, later wrote about this model for gene

Bacterial Viruses and Genetics

Bacteriophages (bacterial viruses) are simple organisms that enter a host bacterium, replicate, and burst the cell in order to complete their life cycle.

A bacteriophage is made from a protein envelope, called a capsid, surrounding a core of genetic material. Bacteriophages infect bacteria by injecting their genetic information into them through hollow protein tubes called tails. The structure of a tail is similar to the structure of a hypodermic needle, which is used to inject medication. Tail fibers on the outside of the bacteriophage help stabilize it during the injection process.

Each type of bacterium has a unique group of bacteriophages that may infect it. The efforts of Delbrück and the other scientists of the so-called phage group were concentrated on the bacteriophage of *Escherichia coli* (*E. coli*). The bacteriophage of *E. coli* used by Delbrück has a life cycle of approximately thirty minutes.

E. coli is a common intestinal bacterium with a life cycle of about forty minutes. At the end of its life cycle, the bacterial cell divides into two new cells. When grown on a culture plate for many generations, bacteria will form a smooth layer of cells called a lawn. Delbrück found that if a dilute solution of bacteriophage is spread over the culture plate before many generations have passed, the effect of the bacteriophage infection can be seen in only a few hours. Instead of developing into a smooth layer of cells, the bacterial lawn will contain clear circles, called plaques. These spots appear where bacteria have been killed by bacteriophage infection.

Delbrück refined experiments that showed the life cycle of a bacteriophage to be divided into three stages, called the latent period, the rise period, and the saturation period. Bacteriophages floating free in a solution of bacteria will infect a bacterium by attaching to the side of the cell and injecting their genetic information into the host.

During the latent period, the bacteriophage genetic information is copied by utilizing the host's reproductive machinery to produce hundreds of bacteriophages within the host. The swollen bacterium eventually bursts, and the new bacteriophages are released into the bacterial environment; this portion of the bacteriophage life cycle is the rise period. During the saturation period, the newly formed bacteriophages begin to infect neighboring host bacteria.

Bacteriophages are an important tool in the study of genetics. Their simple structure and short life cycle make them ideal for studying gene mutations and genetic changes in organisms as they become resistant to viral infection.

Bibliography

Stent, Günther S. *Molecular Biology of Bacterial Viruses.* San Francisco, Calif.: W. H. Freeman, 1963.

Flint, Jane. *Viruses.* Burlington, N.C.: Carolina Biological Supply Scientific Publication Department, 1988.

Levine, Arnold J. *Viruses.* New York: W. H. Freeman, 1992.

mutation in his book *What Is Life?* (1944). This publication made Delbrück internationally known and attracted many physicists to genetics after the end of World War II.

Research in America

Delbrück received a second Rockefeller Foundation fellowship in 1937 and moved to the California Institute of Technology (Caltech) in Pasadena to study replication, the copying of genes during cell division. He chose to study bacterial viruses, called bacteriophages, because they are simple organisms.

The hardships of World War II forced him to accept a job at Vanderbilt University in Nashville, Tennessee, as a physics instructor. This position allowed him to continue his virus research. In

1940 he met Salvador Edward Luria, who was conducting similar studies in New York City. Delbrück and Luria collaborated on bacteriophage research. Their paper on the ability of these viruses to cause bacterial mutations is considered the birth of bacterial genetics.

The Phage Group

Delbrück and Luria were joined by Alfred Day Hershey, a biochemist from Washington University in St. Louis, in 1943. These three men formed the core of the "phage group," a collection of scientists dedicated to the study of bacteriophage genetics. The phage group grew to include many scientists in different laboratories. The joint effort resulted in the mapping of the bacteriophage life cycle and a detailed understanding of its individual stages.

The 1969 Nobel Prize in Physiology or Medicine was awarded to Delbrück, Luria, and Hershey for "their discoveries concerning the replication mechanism and the genetic structure of viruses." The primary honor of this award was given to Delbrück because he had turned the study of bacterial genetics into an exact science of precise measurement and quantitative experimentation.

Return to Caltech

Delbrück returned to Caltech in 1947, where he concentrated on the molecular biology of sensory perception until his retirement in 1977. He remained interested in philosophy and poetry until his death from bone marrow cancer on March 9, 1981.

Bibliography

By Delbrück

"Cosmic Rays and the Origin of Species," *Nature*, 1936.

"Radiation and the Hereditary Mechanism," *The American Naturalist*, 1940.

"On the Replication of Deoxyribonucleic Acid (DNA)," *Proceedings of the National Academy of Sciences of the United States of America*, 1954.

Mind from Matter?: An Essay on Evolutionary Epistemology, 1986.

About Delbrück

Cairns, John. *Phage and the Origins of Molecular Biology*. Cold Spring Harbor, N.Y.: Cold Spring Harbor Laboratory of Quantitative Biology, 1966.

Judson, Horace Freeland. *The Eighth Day of Creation*. New York: Simon & Schuster, 1979.

Fisher, Ernest Peter and Carol Lipson. *Thinking About Science*. New York: W. W. Norton, 1988.

(Beth Anne Short)

Gerhard Domagk

Disciplines: Bacteriology, chemistry, medicine, and pharmacology

Contribution: Domagk's discovery of the antimicrobial effects of Prontosil was one of the great milestones in the history of medicine.

Oct. 30, 1895	Born in Lagow, Brandenburg, Germany
1915–1918	Serves in the German medical corps
1921	Earns an M.D. from the University of Kiel
1924	Lecturer at the University of Greifswald
1925	Lecturer at the University of Münster
1927	Takes a position at I. G. Farben
1927	Initiates a systematic search for antibacterial chemical substances
1932	Discovers the antibacterial effects of Prontosil
1937	Receives the Emil Fischer Medal of the German Chemical Society
1939	Awarded the Nobel Prize in Physiology or Medicine, but not allowed to accept
1947	Receives his Nobel Medal
1956	Awarded the Paul Ehrlich Gold Medal of the University of Frankfurt
1959	Elected to the Royal Society of London
1960	Given the Order of the Rising Sun by the Japanese government
Apr. 24, 1964	Dies in Burgberg, West Germany

Early Life

Gerhard Johannes Paul Domagk (pronounced "DOH-mahkh"), the son of a teacher, attended an elementary school that emphasized the sciences. After completing secondary school, he began his medical training at the University of Kiel just before the eruption of World War I.

When war came to Europe in 1914, Domagk enlisted in the German army. After recovering from a 1915 battle wound, he was transferred to the medical corps. His experience in trying to treat wounds and infectious diseases with the inadequate therapies of the period undoubtedly influenced the course of his later research.

Resuming his studies at Kiel after the war, Domagk received his medical degree in 1921. He remained there, working as an assistant in the chemistry and pathology departments. In 1924 he assumed the position of lecturer of pathological anatomy at the University of Greifswald; he moved to a similar position at the University of Münster

The Sulfa Drugs and Antibacterial Chemotherapy

Prontosil was the first of the sulfa drugs (also known as the sulfonamides), the first synthetic compounds demonstrated to be both safe and effective against bacterial infections.

After Domagk's 1935 announcement of the effectiveness of Prontosil against streptococcal infections, studies were undertaken in several countries to determine the effects of the drug on diseases caused by other bacteria. Researchers soon found that Prontosil could bring under control meningitis, pneumonia, and gonorrhea.

The drug's success led to the synthesis of other sulfa drugs, some of which were even more potent microbe fighters than Prontosil, and cheaper to manufacture. By 1939 these drugs had assumed a major role in clinical medicine.

The action of sulfa drugs is primarily bacteriostatic. They inhibit bacterial growth by interfering with the utilization of paraminobenzoic acid, a growth factor essential for most bacteria. By preventing the reproduction of susceptible microbes, the drugs give the body's natural defenses the opportunity to destroy disease-causing bacteria.

The advent of the sulfa drugs inaugurated a new era of medicine. Their widespread use resulted in a drastic reduction in deaths from infectious diseases. Before penicillin became widely available in the mid-1940s, the sulfa drugs were the mainstay of antibacterial chemotherapy. Even after the debut of the antibiotics, they continued to occupy a significant, albeit small, niche in medicine.

Bibliography

Galdston, Iago. *Behind the Sulfa Drugs.* New York: Appleton-Century, 1943.

Sokoloff, Boris. *The Miracle Drugs.* New York: Ziff-Davis, 1949.

Schnitzer, Robert J. and Frank Hawking, eds. *Experimental Chemotherapy.* Vol. 2. New York: Academic Press, 1964.

Hedgecock, Lloyd W. *Antimicrobial Agents.* Philadelphia, Pa.: Lea & Febiger, 1967.

in 1925. In the same year, he married Gertrud Strube, with whom he would have a daughter and three sons.

Experiments with Prontosil

In 1927 Domagk went to work for the German chemical firm I. G. Farben as director of the company's research laboratory for experimental pathology and bacteriology. He held that post until his retirement from the company in 1958.

At I. G. Farben, Domagk undertook a systematic investigation of the antimicrobial effects of thousands of chemical compounds, including the new synthetic dyes. In 1932 he tested an orange-red leather dye that carried the trade name of Prontosil. Around Christmastime, 1932, Domagk made a momentous discovery: the Prontosil dye protected laboratory mice against lethal streptococcal infections.

He soon found that the compound had a similar effect on infected humans. One of the first human recipients of Prontosil was Domagk's young daughter, Hildegard, who was suffering from a life-threatening streptococcal infection. Traditional therapies were not helping her. In desperation, Domagk gave her a large dose of Prontosil. She recovered dramatically.

In early 1935 the world learned of the therapeutic benefits of Prontosil when Domagk published his findings in a German medical journal. Domagk's discovery of the antibacterial activity of Prontosil revolutionized bacterial chemotherapy. His achievement earned for him the 1939 Nobel Prize in Physiology or Medicine. He was forced to decline the award, however, because of Nazi policy. He eventually received his Nobel Medal in 1947.

Other Research Interests

Domagk also engaged in research on tuberculosis and cancer. His work on antitubercular compounds, which began during World War II, resulted in some drugs of limited use against the disease, although the group of compounds that he investigated turned out to be somewhat toxic.

During the mid-1950s, Domagk became increasingly interested in the chemotherapy of malignant tumors. After his retirement from I. G. Farben, he engaged in cancer research at the University of Münster. Domagk spent the last few years of his scientific career searching, without success, for an anticancer drug. He died in 1964.

Bibliography

By Domagk

"Ein Beitrag zur Chemotherapie der bakteriellen Infektionen," *Deutsche medizinische Wochenschrift*, 1935.

Pathologische Anatomie und Chemotherapie der Infektionskrankheiten, 1947.

Chemotherapie der Tuberkulose mit den Thiosemikarbazonen, 1950.

About Domagk

Gillispie, Charles Coulston, ed. *Dictionary of Scientific Biography*. New York: Charles Scribner's Sons, 1970.

Wasson, Tyler, ed. *Nobel Prize Winners: An H. W. Wilson Biographical Dictionary*. New York: H. W. Wilson, 1987.

Magill, Frank N., ed. *The Nobel Prize Winners: Physiology or Medicine*. Pasadena, Calif.: Salem Press, 1991.

McMurray, Emily J., ed. *Notable Twentieth-Century Scientists*. Detroit, Mich.: Gale Research, 1995.

(*Ronald W. Long*)

Renato Dulbecco

Disciplines: Biology and genetics
Contribution: Dulbecco's discoveries concerned the interaction of tumor viruses and animal cells, which is essential to an understanding of cancer.

Feb. 22, 1914	Born in Catanzaro, Italy
1936	Receives an M.D. from the University of Turin
1936	Enters the Italian army as a medical officer
1942	Hospitalized for several months with a serious wound during World War II
1947	Emigrates to the United States to work with Salvador Luria
1952	Associate professor of biology at the California Institute of Technology (Caltech)
1953	Becomes a U.S. citizen
1955	Full professor at Caltech
1963	Senior Research Fellow at the Salk Institute
1972	Named assistant director of the British Imperial Cancer Fund
1975	Shares the Nobel Prize in Physiology or Medicine with David Baltimore and Howard M. Temin
1977	Named distinguished research professor at the Salk Institute
1982	President of the Salk Institute
1992	Retires
Feb. 20, 2012	Dies in San Diego, California

Early Life

Renato Dulbecco (pronounced "duhl-BEH-koh") was born in Catanzaro, Italy, to Leonardo Dulbecco, a civil engineer, and Maria Virdia Dulbecco. The family moved to Turin and Cineo, in northern Italy, when Leonardo was drafted during World War I. Later, they relocated to Imperia, where Renato attended primary and secondary school. Precocious and brilliant in physics, he built one of the first electronic seismographs.

At sixteen, Dulbecco entered the University of Turin's premedical program. By the end of freshman year, he was fascinated by biology and began working with Professor Guisseppe Levi, an anatomist and nerve tissue expert. Dulbecco learned histology, the microscopic study of tissue anatomy, and culture techniques for growing cells. He also befriended future Nobel laureates Salvador Edward Luria and Rita Levi-Montalcini, who later influenced his career.

Medicine, the Military, and America

In 1936 Dulbecco received his M.D. and was drafted as an army physician. He was discharged in 1938 and recalled in 1939. The following year, Dulbecco married Guiseppina Salvo. They had a son, Peter Leonardo, and a daughter, Maria Vittoria. During World War II, from 1940 to 1942, Dulbecco was a physician in France and Russia. Wounded badly in Russia, he was hospitalized for several months in 1942. On returning home, he became the physician for Italian partisans resisting German occupation.

After World War II, Dulbecco became a Turin city councilor but gave up politics in 1946 to conduct research at the University of Turin as a professor of embryology. Then, Luria, a faculty member at the University of Indiana at Bloomington, invited Dulbecco to join him. Dulbecco soon moved to the United States; he became a citizen in 1953.

From Work with Viruses to Greatness

With Luria, Dulbecco began the study of bacteriophages (or phages)—viruses that destroy bacteria. Soon, the eminent scientist Max Delbrück offered him a senior research fellowship at the California Institute of Technology (Caltech). Success led Dulbecco to become a Caltech associate professor of biology in 1952 and a full professor in 1954. He continued his work on phages until the 1960s, when he began to study the animal viruses that cause diseases such as polio and cancer.

Much of Dulbecco's work explored polyoma virus, which causes multiple tumors in mice, and simian virus 40, which causes leukemia in monkeys. Among his most important discoveries was that the transformation of normal cells to cancer cells by tumor viruses involves viral hereditary information and causes the ability of the cells to divide rapidly and repeatedly. This ability is absent in normal cells, which divide slowly.

In 1963 Dulbecco joined the Salk Institute in La Jolla, California. After a divorce, he married Maureen Muir, and they had a daughter. Dulbecco remained at the institute until 1972, when Britain's Imperial Cancer Fund made him its assistant director.

In 1975 he shared the Nobel Prize in Physiology or Medicine with Howard M. Temin and David Baltimore for the study of the interaction of tumor viruses and cell genetic material. In his Nobel lecture, Dulbecco urged society to stop making substances that cause cancer and polluting the world with them.

Later Years

After 1977 Dulbecco was named distinguished research professor at the Salk Institute, continued to conduct research, and won more honors and prizes. Honorary degrees came from Yale and the University of Glasgow, and the prizes included the Lasker Basic Medical Research Award, the Waksman Award from the National Academy of Sciences, and the Mandai Gold Medal from the Czechoslovakian Academy of Sciences. Dulbecco also became a member of the National Academy of Sciences and the Royal Society of London. He served as president of the Salk Institute from 1982 until 1992, when he retired.

Bibliography

By Dulbecco
The Induction of Cancer by Viruses, 1967.
Induction of Host Systems, Integration and Excision, 1975.
The Design of Life, 1987.
Virology, 1980 (with Harold S. Ginsberg; originally section of *Microbiology*, 1967, ed. Bernard D. Davis et al.).

About Dulbecco
McGraw-Hill Modern Scientists and Engineers. McGraw-Hill, 1980.
Nobel Lectures: Physiology or Medicine. World Scientific Publishing, 1992.
Magill, Frank N., ed. "Renato Dulbecco," *The Nobel Prize Winners: Physiology or Medicine*, Pasadena, Calif.: Salem Press, 1991.

(Sanford S. Singer)

Viruses and Cancer

Some viruses can transform animal cells to cancer cells via deoxyribonucleic acid (DNA) oncogenes.

The viral ribonucleic acid (RNA) of retroviruses, so-named because their reverse transcriptases turn RNA to DNA and add it to the DNA of infected cells, can cause cancer. Each time that an infected cell duplicates, a viral "oncogene" (cancer-causing gene) is created. In 1975 Dulbecco, Howard M. Temin, and David Baltimore won the Nobel Prize in Physiology or Medicine for explaining this concept. Temin and Baltimore identified the retroviruses and reverse transcriptases, respectively, and Dulbecco began with viruses (phages) that infect and kill bacteria. His main phage discovery was that white light reverses the ultraviolet (UV) light inactivation caused by phages.

Dulbecco developed methods to count animal viruses in cell cultures. The plaque assay counts plaques (clear spots) where viruses have killed infected cells. Next, he examined viruses thought to cause animal cancer, especially mouse polyoma virus. The study of this virus showed viral DNA combining with afflicted (host) cell DNA and being reproduced generation after generation. Transformed host cells quickly reproduce, over and over, causing a tumorlike mass. This rapid reproduction differs from the slow reproduction of normal cells.

Bibliography

Dulbecco, Renato. *Induction of Cancer by Viruses.* New York: W. H. Freeman, 1967.
Dulbecco, Renato. *Induction of Host Systems, Integration and Excision.* Cambridge, England: Cambridge University Press, 1975.
Dulbecco, Renato. *The Design of Life.* New Haven, Conn.: Yale University Press, 1987.

Paul Ehrlich

Disciplines: Bacteriology, cell biology, chemistry, immunology, medicine, and pharmacology

Contribution: Ehrlich developed important stains, produced an antitoxin for diphtheria, and inspired both praise and controversy for his development of a drug to treat syphilis.

Mar. 14, 1854	Born in Strehlen, Silesia, Prussia (now Strzelin in Poland)
1878	Earns an M.D. from the University of Breslau
1878	Joins the clinic at the Charité Hospital in Berlin
1882	Begins research with Robert Koch on the microorganism that causes tuberculosis
1886	Develops methylene blue, a selective stain for nerves
1887-1889	Diagnosed with tuberculosis and lives in Egypt
1889	Begins work for Koch at the Institute for Infectious Diseases
1891	Professor at the University of Berlin
1892	Introduces an improved antitoxin for diphtheria
1896	Director of the State Institute for the Investigation and Control of Sera
1899	Named director of the Institute for Experimental Therapy
1908	Awarded the Nobel Prize in Physiology or Medicine 1910
Aug. 20, 1915	Dies in Bad Homburg, Germany

Early Life

Paul Ehrlich (pronounced "AYR-lihk") was born in 1854 in Strehlen, Silesia, Prussia (now in Poland), into a notable Jewish family. His father, Ismar Ehrlich, was an innkeeper, and his mother, Rosa Weigert, was the aunt of bacteriologist Karl Weigert. Paul was somewhat eccentric, like his father, and, although he did not perform well in school, he developed a strong interest in both chemistry and biology.

Ehrlich attended several universities—Breslau, Strasbourg, Freiburg im Breisgau, and Leipzig—before earning a medical degree at the University of Breslau in 1878. During his studies, he began to experiment with dyes that could be used to stain particular cells and microorganisms. His dissertation described various staining methods for bacteria.

A "Miracle Drug" to Fight Syphilis

Ehrlich's development of compound 606, also known as Salvarsan or arsphenamine, revolutionized medical treatment and offered the first sign of hope against a dreaded disease.

Ehrlich's knowledge of the methods and meaning of cell staining led him to develop the modern concept of chemotherapy, a term that he coined for the creation of chemical compounds to treat disease. He suspected that a stain colors some cells and not others because the dye reacts with certain substances in the targeted cells. He also noted that stains often kill those cells they color. He reasoned that a chemical compound could be created to seek out and kill bacteria or other harmful microorganisms while passing over healthy, normal cells—a so-called magic bullet.

Applying this concept, in 1904 he discovered trypan red, a dye that helped destroy the trypanosomes that cause sleeping sickness. Ehrlich also began studying the effects of atoxyl on trypanosome infection and found that the drug was toxic to the optic nerve, sometimes resulting in blindness.

Ehrlich abandoned atoxyl but learned that some arsenic compounds had promising therapeutic qualities. He and his team of assistants initiated a systematic survey of all arsenic-containing organic compounds. Number 606 in this survey did not prove valuable against trypanosomes and was shelved, but Japanese bacteriologist Sahachiro Hata, who had traveled to Germany to work with Ehrlich, came across it again when asked to determine whether any of the compounds were effective against syphilis. In 1910 Ehrlich confirmed Hata's tests and declared to the world that compound number 606 was a stable agent that destroyed the microorganisms that cause syphilis.

Syphilis is a sexually transmitted disease that in Ehrlich's day was rarely discussed openly but greatly feared. It caused a high fever, intense headaches, skin lesions, and unbearable pain as the disease slowly destroyed the brain and cardiovascular system, often driving victims insane. In untreated cases, syphilis was eventually fatal. It was not until 1905 that the causative agent was identified: the spirochete *Treponema pallidum.*

Prior to 1910, the only treatment available was mercury or potassium iodide. The side effects of large amounts of mercury included severe mouth ulcers, swollen gums, loose teeth, and foul odor. Ehrlich named his new drug Salvarsan, which also became known as arsphenamine. While not an ideal drug because of the need for precise administration and often for repeated doses, it represented a vast improvement in treatment. Ehrlich worked to create an even better compound; he patented neosalvarsan in 1912 and sodium salvarsan in 1913 but did not live to see the realization of his his goal: a drug that cured in a single dose.

Bibliography

Bulloch, William. *The History of Bacteriology.* 1938. Reprint. London: Oxford University Press, 1960.

Taylor, F. Sherwood. "The Rise of Chemotherapy," *The Conquest of Bacteria.* New York: Philosophical Library, 1942.

Galdston, Iago. "The Saga of Salvarsan," *Behind the Sulfa Drugs: A Short History of Chemotherapy.* New York: D. Appleton-Century, 1943.

Reinfeld, Fred. *Miracle Drugs and the New Age of Medicine.* New York: Sterling, 1957.

The Use of Stains

Many of Ehrlich's successes can be traced back to his expertise in staining techniques and in his interpretation of the reactions between dyes and biological materials.

As a student, Ehrlich had already used stains to identify mast cells, which are large cells in connective tissue that release chemicals causing allergic reactions. After his graduation, he began work with Friedrich von Frerichs at the Charité Hospital in Berlin, where he stained a variety of white blood cells and developed methylene blue, a selective stain for the ganglia and endings of nerves.

Fighting Tuberculosis

Ehrlich also studied tuberculosis, a chronic and highly infectious lung disease. Renowned bacteriologist Robert Koch had isolated the tubercle bacillus that causes the disease, and Ehrlich later developed a staining technique for that microorganism to aid in diagnosis. In 1882 they started a collaboration on the etiology (cause) and possible treatment of tuberculosis. The next year, Ehrlich married Hedwig Pinkus; they would have two daughters, Stephanie and Marianne.

Unfortunately, Ehrlich's work with tuberculosis had a price: He contracted a mild case of the disease in 1887 and was forced to move to Egypt for a few years. He soon recovered and never suffered a recurrence, perhaps as a result of Koch's new tuberculin treatment but more likely because of the warm, dry Egyptian climate.

Research in Bacteriology

After his return to Germany, Ehrlich set up his own laboratory to continue his studies of bacteria and other microorganisms. Koch soon offered him a position at the new Institute for Infectious Diseases, and Ehrlich also received a professorship at the University of Berlin.

Ehrlich began another fruitful collaboration, this time with Emil Adolf von Behring and Shibasaburo Kitasato, on a cure for diphtheria, a contagious disease causing the formation of a membrane in the throat and the inflammation of the heart and nervous system. They employed the principles of passive immunity—injection with antibodies from animals inoculated with the microorganisms that cause the disease—in order to create a vaccine (or antitoxin or serum) to cure those infected and prevent the contraction of diphtheria in those exposed. They calculated a safe, effective dosage of the vaccine and conducted successful clinical trials.

Ehrlich pursued his study of antibody formation in the presence of toxins. He developed the side-chain theory, which states that one of the chemical groups in a toxin molecule aligns the molecule with specific receptors, or sidechains, on cells in order to bind to them. For his contributions to bacteriology and immunology, Ehrlich shared the 1908 Nobel Prize in Physiology or Medicine with Élie Metchnikoff.

Salvarsan, Acclaim, and Controversy

Ehrlich spent the rest of his career investigating the design of chemical compounds to treat disease, known as chemotherapy. He determined that arsenic-containing compounds have promising therapeutic qualities and initiated a survey of all such compounds. In 1910 he announced that compound number 606 destroys spirochetes, the microorganisms causing syphilis.

Ehrlich named his new drug Salvarsan; it also became known as arsphenamine. Although more than one dose was often required, it could cure syphilis, a painful and fatal sexually transmitted disease that had plagued humankind for centuries. Ehrlich's discovery was greeted with acclaim within the scientific community, and he was nominated for another Nobel Prize in both 1912 and 1913. Those infected with the disease were given hope, though keeping up with the demand for the drug was difficult.

Ehrlich championed the proper administration of Salvarsan, but controversy arose nevertheless. Some people objected to the concept of a cure for a disease they associated with divine punishment for sin. Others asserted that the drug did not live up to Ehrlich's claims or was misused. In March 1914 the matter was put before the Reichstag (the German legislature), which declared Salvarsan effective. In May of that year, with Ehrlich as a witness in the case, Frankfurt Hospital won a libel suit against a newspaper which claimed that prostitutes had been forced to take the drug.

Ill health, controversy, and the beginning of World War I took their toll on Ehrlich: he suffered a stroke at the end of 1914 and another one the following year. He died on August 20, 1915, at the age of sixty-one.

Bibliography

By Ehrlich

Experimentelle Untersuchungen über Immunität, 1891.

"On Immunity with Special Reference to Cell Life," *Proceedings of the Royal Society*, 1900.

"The Mutual Relations Between Toxin and Antitoxin," *Boston Medical and Surgical Journal*, 1904.

"Physical Chemistry v. Biology in the Doctrine of Immunity," *Boston Medical and Surgical Journal*, 1904.

"Cytotoxins and Cytotoxic Immunity," *Boston Medical and Surgical Journal*, 1904.

Gesammelte Arbeiten zur Immunitätsforschung, 1904 (*Collected Studies on Immunity*, 1906).

Allgemeines über Chemotherapie, 1910.

"Die Behandlung der Syphilis mit dem Ehrlichschen Präparat 606," *Verhandlungen der Gesellschaft Deutscher Naturforscher und Ärzte*, 1910.

Collected Papers, 1956 (3 vols.).

About Ehrlich

Marks, Marguerite. "Paul Ehrlich: The Man and His Works," *McClure's Magazine* 36 (December, 1910).

Marquardt, Martha. *Paul Ehrlich*. New York: Henry Schuman, 1951.

Jokl, Ernst. "Paul Ehrlich—Man and Scientist," *Bulletin of the New York Academy of Sciences* 30 (1954).

Browning, Carl H. "Emil Behring and Paul Ehrlich: Their Contributions to Science," *Nature* 175 (April, 1955).

Magill, Frank N., ed. "Paul Ehrlich," *The Nobel Prize Winners: Physiology or Medicine*, Pasadena, Calif.: Salem Press, 1991.

(Tracy Irons-Georges)

Sir Alexander Fleming

Discipline: Bacteriology

Contribution: Fleming was awarded the Nobel Prize in Physiology or Medicine for discovering penicillin, an antibiotic that led to a revolution in medical care.

Aug. 6, 1881	Born in Lochfield, Ayrshire, Scotland
1908	Earns a bachelor of medicine degree at London University
1909	Fellow of the Royal College of Surgeons of England
1919	Named Hunterian Professor of the Royal College of Surgeons
1928	Discovers the antibacterial effect of *Penicillium notatum*
1928	Professor of bacteriology at St. Mary's Hospital Medical School, London University
1929	Publishes a paper on the antibacterial action of *Penicillium*
1932	President of the pathology section of the Royal Society of Medicine
1943	Fellow of the Royal Society of London
1945	Awarded the Nobel Prize in Physiology or Medicine
1945	Awarded the Louis Pasteur Medal
1946	Given the Gold Medal of the Royal College of Surgeons
1947	Awarded the Gold Medal of the Royal Society of Medicine
Mar. 11, 1955	Dies in London, England

Early Life

Alexander Fleming was the son of a farmer in the Scottish lowlands. At the age of thirteen, after attending several country schools, Fleming moved to London, where he took courses at the Regent Street Polytechnic School. He began his scientific career in 1901, after a small inheritance enabled him to attend St. Mary's Medical School in London.

St. Mary's Medical School

Fleming was a prize-winning student and a superb technician. He qualified as a doctor in 1908 and remained at St. Mary's as a junior assistant to Almroth Edward Wright, a prominent pathologist and well-known proponent of inoculation. During World War I, Wright and Fleming joined the Royal Army Medical Corps in France, where they conducted wound research at a laboratory in Boulogne. Fleming was in charge of identifying the infecting bacteria by taking swabs from wounds before, during, and after surgery.

The horrors of bacterial infection during World War I had a lasting impact on Fleming, who decided to focus his postwar research on antibiotic substances. He was convinced that the ideal antiseptic (bacteria-fighting) agent should be highly active against microorganisms but harmless to the body's own white blood cell defenses.

Penicillin

In September, 1928, Fleming noticed that a mold was growing in a petri dish containing strains of staphylococci and that the bacteria surrounding the mold were being destroyed. It is likely that the source of the mold spores was the laboratory below that of Fleming, where mycologist (mold expert) C. J. La Touche was growing molds for research on allergies.

Because of his interest in antibiotics, Fleming was conditioned to recognize immediately that an agent capable of dissolving staphylococci could be of great biological significance. He preserved the original culture plate and made a subculture of the mold in a tube of broth. Fleming's mold was later identified as *Penicillium notatum.* Further experiments showed that the "mould juice" could be produced by several strains of *Penicillium* but not by other molds. The substance was nontoxic and did not interfere with the action of white blood cells.

Fleming described his findings in a paper entitled "On the Antibacterial Action of Cultures of a *Penicillium,* with Special Reference to Their Use in the Isolation of *B. Influenzae,*" which appeared in the *British Journal of Experimental Pathology* in 1929. The unusual title refers to Fleming's use of penicillin to isolate *B. influenzae,* a bacteria that was not vulnerable to penicillin.

His paper described the mold extract and listed the sensitive bacteria. Most importantly, Fleming suggested that penicillin might be used in the treatment of infection. In addition to describing his experiments, Fleming also stated that the name "penicillin" would be used to describe the mold broth filtrate. His description of penicillin has since been regarded as one of the most important medical papers ever written.

During 1929, Fleming continued to investigate the antibiotic properties of penicillin, collecting data that clearly established its chemotherapeutic potential. Fleming was unable to purify and concentrate penicillin adequately and hence did not conduct clinical tests that proved the effectiveness of the antibiotic in vivo (within a living organism). The significance of Fleming's discovery was not recognized until 1940, when Howard Florey and Ernst B. Chain discovered the enormous therapeutic power of penicillin.

Awards

Once the benefits of penicillin became appreciated, Fleming received many awards for his work, including the 1945 Nobel Prize in Physiology or Medicine, jointly with Florey and Chain, the Louis Pasteur Medal in 1945, the Gold Medal of the Royal College of Surgeons in 1946, and the Gold Medal of the Royal Society of Medicine in 1947. He was knighted in 1944 and named a commander of the French Legion of Honor in 1945.

Sir Alexander Fleming died on March 11, 1955, in London at the age of seventy-three.

Bibliography

By Fleming

"On the Bacteriology of Septic Wounds," *The Lancet,* 1915.

"The Action of Chemical and Physiological Antiseptics in a Septic Wound," *British Journal of Surgery,* 1919.

"On a Remarkable Bacteriolytic Element Found in Tissues and Secretions," *Proceedings of the Royal Society,* 1922.

"A Comparison of the Activities of Antiseptics on Bacteria and Leucocytes," *Proceedings of the Royal Society,* 1924.

Penicillin

Penicillin is an antibiotic isolated from the Penicillium notatum, *a common blue-green mold. Discovered by Fleming in 1928, penicillin led to a revolution in the treatment of diseases caused by bacteria.*

During the nineteenth and early twentieth centuries, scientists could isolate bacteria but were uncertain as to the best method for combating these disease-causing organisms. Antiseptics were a known means for killing bacteria, but they could not be used internally and were not always effective, especially when applied in deep wounds.

Fleming and his mentor, Almroth Edward Wright, showed that white blood cells found in the pus discharged from wounds had ingested bacteria. They also knew that antiseptics destroyed the body's own defenses (white blood cells), allowing the remaining bacteria to create serious infections unimpeded. Fleming's work on infected wounds during World War I inspired him to begin searching for nontoxic antibiotics.

In September, 1928, while examining a stack of petri dishes prior to cleaning them, Fleming discovered the antibiotic properties of *Penicillium notatum*. He was unable to establish the clinical effectiveness of penicillin, however, and, by 1931, had shifted his antibiotic research to sulfa drugs.

Nine years later, Howard Florey and Ernst B. Chain succeeded in concentrating and clinically testing penicillin. As a result, Fleming became one of the best-known scientists of the twentieth century and was showered with accolades and honors. Penicillin achieved particular notoriety during World War II because of the demand for an antibiotic that could halt scourges such as gas gangrene, which had infected the wounds of numerous soldiers during World War I.

With the help of Florey's and Chain's Oxford group, scientists at the U.S. Department of Agriculture's Northern Regional Research Laboratory developed a highly efficient method for mass-producing penicillin, using fermentation. The same group also isolated a more productive *Penicillium* strain (*Penicillium chrysogenum*). By 1945, a strain was developed that produced 500 times more penicillin than Fleming's original mold. During World War II, the Committee on Medical Research, of the U.S. Office of Scientific Research and Development (OSRD), conducted large-scale clinical tests of penicillin on 10,838 patients. Their results provided doctors with effective methods and dosages for the use of penicillin in the treatment of many diseases.

Penicillin has since been regarded as among the greatest medical discoveries of the twentieth century. Practically every organ in the body is vulnerable to bacteria. Before penicillin, the only antimicrobial drugs available were quinine, arsenic, and sulfa drugs. Of these, only the sulfa drugs were useful for the treatment of bacterial infection, and in many cases high toxicity precluded their use. With this limited arsenal, doctors were helpless as thousands died in epidemics caused by bacteria. Fleming's discovery and the work of Florey and Chain provided a cure for scourges such as pneumonia, meningitis, gas gangrene, and syphilis.

Penicillin and other antibiotics also had a broad impact on medicine as major operations such as heart surgery, organ transplantation, and the management of severe burns became possible once the threat of bacterial infection was minimized. Penicillin led to a revolution in medical treatment by offering an extremely effective solution to infectious disease.

Bibliography

Fleming, Alexander. "On the Antibacterial Action of Cultures of a *Penicillium,* with Special Reference to Their Use in Isolation of *B. Influenzae,*" *British Journal of Experimental Pathology* 10 (1929).

Hare, Ronald. *The Birth of Penicillin and the Disarming of Microbes.* London: Allen and Unwin, 1970.

Macfarlane, Gwyn. *Alexander Fleming: The Man and the Myth.* Cambridge, Mass.: Harvard University Press, 1984.

"On the Antibacterial Action of Cultures of a
Penicillium, with Special Reference to Their
Use in the Isolation of *B. Influenzae*," *British
Journal of Experimental Pathology* 10, 1929.

About Fleming

Maurois, André. *The Life of Alexander Fleming.*
New York: E. P. Dutton, 1959.

Hare, Ronald. *The Birth of Penicillin and the
Disarming of Microbes.* London: Allen and
Unwin, 1970.

Macfarlane, Gwyn. *Alexander Fleming: The Man
and the Myth.* Cambridge, Mass.: Harvard
University Press, 1984.

Hobby, Gladys L. *Penicillin, Meeting the Challenge.*
New Haven, Conn.: Yale University Press, 1985.

(Peter Neushul)

George Herbert Hitchings, Jr.

Disciplines: Biology, chemistry, medicine,
and pharmacology

Contribution: Hitchings, one of the most
successful twentieth-century practitioners of
chemotherapy, introduced rational drug design
and many pharmaceuticals to medical use.

Apr. 18, 1905	Born in Hoquiam, Washington
1927	Receives a B.S. in chemistry at the University of Washington
1928	Earns an M.S. in chemistry from Washington
1933	Receives a Ph.D. in biological chemistry from Harvard University
1942	Hired by Burroughs Wellcome pharmaceutical company
1951	Develops the anticarcinogen 6-mercaptopurine
1957	Develops the drug azothioprine (Immuran), which is widely used as an immunosuppressant in organ transplantation
1967	Vice president of research at Burroughs Wellcome
1971	Becomes president of the Burroughs Wellcome Fund
1975	Retires to become scientist emeritus for the company
1977	Develops the drug acyclovir (Zovirax)
1988	Awarded, with Gertrude Belle Elion and James Whyte Black, the Nobel Prize in Physiology or Medicine
Feb. 27, 1998	Died in Chapel Hill, North Carolina

Early Life

George Herbert Hitchings, Jr., was born on April 18, 1905. The slow death of his father, a naval architect, when Hitchings was twelve, aimed him toward medicine. Another force in this direction was his awe for scientist and philanthropist Louis Pasteur, as described in Hitchings' high school salutatorian address.

Hitchings entered the University of Washington premedical track. He changed to chemistry, though, and received a B.S. and an M.S. in chemistry in 1927 and 1928, respectively. A well-rounded student, he also took arts and history courses.

From Harvard to Pharmaceuticals

Hitchings entered Harvard University's Ph.D. program in biological chemistry and worked with Cyrus J. Fiske on nucleic acids, before James D. Watson and Francis Crick showed that deoxyribonucleic acid (DNA) contains hereditary information. Hitchings' Ph.D. thesis, leading to a

degree in 1933, concerned nucleic acid chemistry. That year, he married Beverly Reimer. They had two children, Laramie Ruth and Thomas Eldridge.

The Great Depression forced Hitchings to teach for the next nine years. In 1942 he was hired by the U.S. division of the British pharmaceutical company Burroughs Wellcome, started its biochemistry department, and soon hired Gertrude Belle Elion. He continued to study nucleic acids, which led him to a vice presidency in research in 1967. He held that job until retirement in 1975.

Rational Drug Design and a Nobel Prize

Hitchings' fame arose from work done with Gertrude Elion. They pioneered pharmaceutical identification by rational drug design. The first stage of this process exposes the differences between abnormal (for example, infected or cancerous) tissue and normal tissue, and the second stage exploits those differences to kill abnormal cells and to affect normal ones only minimally. Rational drug design differs from screening, which tests available chemicals for useful drugs. Hitchings and his co-workers were prolific, earning approximately 100 patents in a thirty-year association.

Many such drugs were synthetic bases—cousins of the bases in nucleic acids. Chemical alteration of natural prototypes yielded drugs that diminished or stopped the key steps of DNA synthesis and were excreted rapidly. These properties are useful in treating cancer, because cancer cells divide much more rapidly than normal cells. Hence, they are killed quickly by DNA starvation, while slow-dividing normal cells are affected to a lesser degree before the drugs are excreted.

The first drug designed by Hitchings, in 1951, was the anticarcinogen 6-mercaptopurine, which is still in wide use. A second drug, azothioprine (Immuran), made in 1957, slows the division of white blood cells of the immune system. Immuran, a widely used immunosuppressant, enables high

Rational Drug Design

Rational drug design develops pharmaceuticals via the scientific study of life processes.

The use of rational drug design led Hitchings' group to the development of approximately 100 pharmaceuticals, mostly modified nucleic acid bases. His premises were that suitable drugs kill abnormal cells or microbes with minimal harm to normal tissue, and that every cell type has a unique biochemistry allowing attack at a point crucial to its survival and reproduction.

Hitchings' modified nucleic acid bases inhibited the synthesis of nucleic acid, especially deoxyribonucleic acid (DNA). They were chosen partly because of Hitchings' work with Cyrus Fiske on nucleic acid. Hitching also used modified bases because parasites live in hostile environments and utilize rapid nucleic acid synthesis for survival and because an understanding of the relationship between heredity and nucleic acid was emerging.

Hitchings' system of rational drug design produced chemotherapeutic bases, including immunosuppressants and drugs to fight leukemia, gout, virus, and acquired immunodeficiency syndrome (AIDS). It soon became the model for drug research.

Bibliography

Talalay, Paul. "Presentation of Dr. George Herbert Hitchings for Passano Award," *Journal of the American Medical Association* 209 (September 1, 1969).

Hitchings, George H. "Relevance of Basic Research to Pharmaceutical Inventions," *Trends in Pharmacological Sciences* (1980).

success rates in organ transplantation. A third drug, acyclovir (Zovirax), developed in 1977, was the first antiviral drug and treatment for acquired immunodeficiency syndrome (AIDS). The drugs designed by Hitchings' group treat diseases such as cancer, gout, malaria, and viral infections. It was no wonder that he, Elion, and British pharmacologist James Whyte Black won the 1988 Nobel Prize in Physiology or Medicine.

Hitchings won prizes, honorary degrees, and memberships to learned societies. In addition to the Nobel Prize, he was given the Passano Award, the Gregor Mendel Award of the Czech Academy of Science, and the Papanicolaou Cancer Award. His honorary degrees included those from the University of Michigan, Emory and Duke universities, and Mount Sinai Medical School. Hitchings was elected to the Royal Society of London, the National Academy of Science, and the American Society for Cancer Research.

After Retirement

Upon his retirement, Hitchings continued to conduct research and had more time for philanthropic work. One example is the Burroughs Wellcome Fund, a charitable organization for which he served as president from 1971 to 1990. Retirement also gave him the opportunity to travel extensively, a longtime hobby.

Bibliography

By Hitchings

"The Effect of Pyrimidines on the Growth of *Lactobacillus casei*," Science, 1945 (with E. A. Falco and M. B. Sherwood).

"A Quarter Century of Chemotherapy," *Journal of the American Medical Association*, 1969.

"Indications for Control Mechanisms in Purine and Pyrimidine Biosynthesis as Revealed by Studies with Inhibitors," *Advances in Enzyme Regulation*, 1974.

"Relevance of Basic Research to Pharmaceutical Invention," *Trends in Pharmacological Sciences,* 1980.

"Rational Design of Anticancer Drugs: Here, Imminent, or Illusive?" *Development of Target-Oriented Anticancer Drugs,* 1983 (Yung-Chi Cheng, Barry Goz, and Mimi Minkoff, eds.).

About Hitchings

"George Herbert Hitchings," *Encyclopædia Britannica* online, http://www.britannica.com/EBchecked/topic/267978/George-Herbert-Hitchings

Talalay, Paul. "Presentation of Dr. George Herbert Hitchings for Passano Award," *Journal of the American Medical Association* 209 (September 1, 1969).

Hitchings, George H. "A Quarter Century of Chemotherapy," *Journal of the American Medical Association* (1969).

Bouton, Katherine. "The Nobel Pair," *New York Times Magazine* (January 29, 1989).

(Sanford S. Singer)

Alick Isaacs

Disciplines: Biology and virology

Contribution: Isaacs discovered interferon, a protein that explains why only one ribonucleic acid (RNA) virus type can infect the body at a time.

July 17, 1921	Born in Glasgow, Scotland
1944	Graduated from Glasgow University's faculty of medicine
1945	Becomes McCann Research Scholar in Glasgow's bacteriology department
1947	Receives a Medical Research Council Studentship to attend Sheffield University
1948	Wins a Rockefeller Fellowship to study virology in Australia
1949	Marries Susanna Gordon Foss
1950	Becomes director of the World Influenza Centre at the National Institute for Medical Research (NIMR)
1954	Receives an M.D. from Glasgow University
1957	Describes interferon in two articles
1961	Becomes head of the virology division at NIMR
1966	Elected to the Royal Society of London
Jan. 25, 1967	Dies in London, England

Early Life

Alick Isaacs was born in Glasgow, Scotland, to Louis and Rosine Isaacs. Louis, a merchant-peddler, had four children, of whom Alick was the oldest. Isaacs attended Glasgow public schools and private Hebrew schools. During his teenage years, he became interested in music and chess; these hobbies continued throughout his life.

In 1944 Isaacs was graduated from Glasgow University with an M.B. and a Ch.B. At the university, he won prizes in dermatology and surgery, but he lacked a calling for clinical medicine. Hence, from 1945 to 1947, he served as a McCann Research Scholar in the bacteriology department at Glasgow.

Because of Isaacs' skill in bacteriology, he won a 1947 Medical Research Council Studentship to Sheffield University. There, while working with eminent microbiologists, his interest in influenza (flu) and flu virus began and would be essential to his later career.

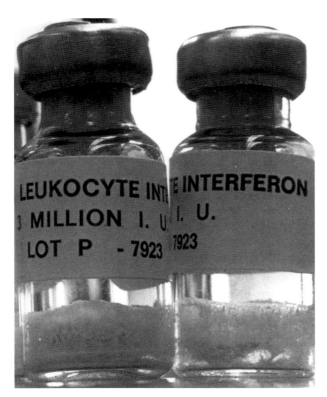

Isaacs discovered interferon proteins, now used to fight viral diseases and cancer.

A Visit to Australia

In 1948 Isaacs won a Rockefeller Fellowship to study viruses for a year at the Eliza Hall Institute in Melbourne, Australia. A Medical Research Council award enabled him to stay another year. Throughout this period, Isaacs studied the flu and the viruses that cause it, the body's response to flu virus, and the viral interference phenomenon, which stops more than one virus from infecting a human or animal at a time.

In 1949 Isaacs married Susanna Gordon Foss. Susanna, a physician, specialized in psychiatry. She and Alick later had twin sons and a daughter. In 1950 they returned to London, where Isaacs directed the World Influenza Centre at the National Institute for Medical Research (NIMR). He guided the identification of flu virus strains and helped pinpoint sites of origin for flu epidemics. He also earned an M.D. from Glasgow University in 1954.

Flu and Interferon

Isaacs' discovery of interferon arose from work on the viral interference phenomenon begun in Australia. He found that interference caused by flu virus was not related to viral penetration of cells during infection. Rather, it appeared to be the result of an event occurring in infected cells.

At NIMR, Isaacs identified the substance interferon in collaborations with visiting Swiss scientist Jean Lindenmann. In 1957 their research culminated in two in vitro observations that were key to the description of interferon. First, the interfering substance was present in the culture fluid that surrounds tissue samples, and, second, infected tissues were stimulated by flu virus to produce the interfering agent—that which Isaacs and Lindenmann named interferon. Next, they showed that interferon either was a protein or required a protein for its biological action.

As Isaacs' work progressed, he received wide recognition from the biomedical community and was asked to head the virology division at NIMR

Interferon

Isaacs helped discover interferon proteins, which fight viral diseases and cancer.

Many communicable diseases, such as colds, influenza (flu), and polio, are caused by viruses containing ribonucleic acid (RNA) hereditary material. Unaffected by antibiotics, they are commonly stopped (when the body's immune system cannot fight them off) via preventive vaccines. It has long been known that only one RNA virus disease can be caught at a time, known as the viral interference phenomenon. Isaacs showed that the protein interferon causes this phenomenon. Although he died in 1967 before his work matured, others have shown how interferon action occurs. Viral RNA enters a cell and causes interferon production. Interferon is released from cells killed by the virus. Other cells come into contact with the released interferon and develop resistance to the virus and most other RNA viruses.

Interferons stop several activities: the conversion of cells to virus factories for RNA and proteins that become new viruses (progeny), the assembly of many progeny, the destruction of cells by the progeny and the entry of each new virus into another cell to restart the process, and repeated infections. Interferons cause cells to make oligoadenylate synthetase (OS) and elf-2 kinase (EK). EK prevents progeny protein synthesis by inactivating factor elf-2. OS causes the production of 2, 5-A, which causes the destruction of viral RNA.

Interferon is too expensive for use against common viral diseases, but it is used to cure viral hepatitis, rabies, and cancers caused by viruses. Although much was done after Isaacs' death, he is accredited as the founder of interferon research.

Bibliography

Edelhart, Mike and Jean Lindenmann. *Interferon, the New Hope for Cancer.* Reading, Mass.: Addison-Wesley 1981.

Baron, Samuel. "Interferon," *McGraw-Hill Encyclopedia of Science and Technology.* New York: McGraw-Hill, 1987.

---

from 1961 to 1965. Throughout his life, his interest in the flu never waned. Isaacs' efforts were lauded as of great importance to the treatment of viral diseases and of potential value to the study of the numerous cancers thought to be caused by viruses.

Premature Death

Isaacs' health failed in 1964, when he suffered an inoperable subarachnoid hemorrhage. After recovering from the hemorrhage, he gave up his job as an NIMR division head but retained control of the Laboratory for Interferon Research. In 1966 he won more acclaim with his election to the Royal Society of London. He then had a fatal recurrence of intracranial hemorrhage, however, and died in London on January 25, 1967, at the age of forty-five.

Bibliography

By Isaacs

"Virus Interference: I. The Interferon," *Proceedings of the Royal Society of London,* 1957 (with Jean Lindenmann).

"Virus Interference: II. Some Properties of the Interferon," *Proceedings of the Royal Society of London,* 1957 (with Lindenmann and R. C. Valentine).

About Isaacs

Andrewes, C. H. "Alick Isaacs," *Biographical Memoirs of the Fellows of the Royal Society* 13 (1967).

Obituary, *Nature* 213 (February 11, 1967).

Dictionary of National Biography. Oxford, England: Oxford University Press, 1982.

(Sanford S. Singer)

François Jacob

Disciplines: Bacteriology, cell biology, genetics, and virology

Contribution: A brilliant theorist, Jacob helped to develop the concepts of messenger RNA and the operon as a model for gene regulation in bacteria.

June 17, 1920	Born in Nancy, France
1947	Receives an M.D. degree
1951	Begins a long collaboration with Élie Wollman, studying the genetic basis of lysogeny
1954	Earns a D.Sc. in science from the Sorbonne in Paris
1956	Laboratory director at the Institut Pasteur
1960	Chair of the cell genetics department at the Institut Pasteur
1960	With Jacques Monod, proposes the operon as a model for gene regulation in bacteria
1962	With Wollman, devises the technique of interrupted mating in bacteria
1964-1991	Professor of cell genetics at the Collège de France
1965	Receives the Nobel Prize in Physiology or Medicine
1973	Named a member of the Royal Society of London
1977	Named a member of the Académie des Sciences, in Paris
1982-1988	Chairman of the Board of the Institut Pasteur
1987	Publishes his autobiography *La Statue intérieure* (*The Statue Within*, 1988)
April 19, 2013	Dies in Paris, France

Early Life

Born in 1920, in Nancy, France, François Jacob (pronounced "zhah-KOHB") grew up with the ambition of becoming a surgeon. In 1940 his medical studies at the Faculté de Paris were interrupted by World War II, and he fought with the French Free Forces in northern Africa. Jacob subsequently completed his medical studies, but he was unable to practice surgery because of injuries that he sustained during the war.

Turning to biology, Jacob joined André Lwoff's laboratory at the Institut Pasteur in 1950. Soon thereafter, he began a long and fruitful collaboration with Élie Wollman, initially working on various genetic aspects of bacteriophage (viral) infection of bacteria. Jacob received the D.Sc. degree from the Sorbonne, in Paris, in 1954 and two years later was appointed as a laboratory director at the Institut Pasteur.

In 1954, Jacob was named laboratory director of the Pasteur Institute.

The Lac-Operon

Genes involved with the metabolism of the sugar lactose are actively expressed only in the presence of the inducer, lactose. In the absence of lactose, the lac-repressor binds to the deoxyribonucleic acid (DNA), inhibiting the expression of the genes.

Jacob and Jacques Monod identified three adjacent structural genes involved in lactose utilization, which share a common regulatory control in a scheme that they termed the "lac-operon." (In the accompanying figures, *i* is the regulatory gene, *p* is the promoter site, *o* is the operator sequence, *z* is the gene encoding β-galactosidase enzyme, *y* is the gene encoding permease enzyme, *a* is the gene encoding transacetylase enzyme, RP is the repressor protein, rnap is the RNA polymerase, and *L* is lactose.) The operon also includes a short DNA sequence called the operator, located immediately "upstream" from gene *z*.

Outside the operon and even further upstream is

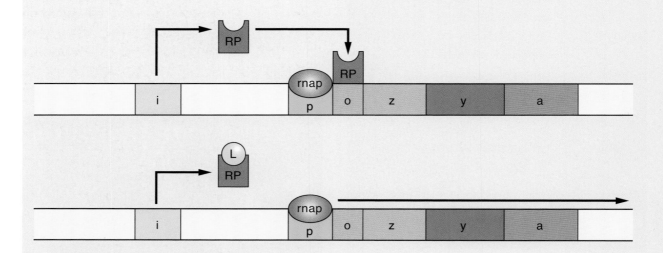

1. In the absence of lactose, the repressor protein binds to the operator, blocking the movement of RNA polymerase. The genes are turned off.
2. When lactose is present, it preferentially binds the repressor protein, freeing up the operator and allowing RNA polymerase to move through the operon. The genes are turned on.

found the regulatory gene, i. Gene i encodes the lac-repressor, a protein that has an affinity for the operator. When the lac-repressor is bound to the operator, it blocks the movement of the enzyme ribonucleic acid (RNA) polymerase, which attaches to the DNA at the upstream promotor. An RNA transcript of the structural genes is thus not made, and the genes are repressed (turned off).

The lac-repressor has a much stronger affinity for lactose, however, than it does for the operator. In the presence of lactose, it will leave the operator to bind to lactose, thus allowing RNA polymerase to make messenger RNA (mRNA) copies of the structural genes. All lac enzymes will be produced until the lactose is finally exhausted, at which time the lac-repressor can again bind to the operator to shut down mRNA synthesis.

Gene regulation is a complex process that can occur at several levels in the cell. The lac-operon was the first regulatory mechanism to be described in detail and serves as the model for many subsequent studies.

Bibliography

Beckwith, J. R. and D. Zipser, eds. *The Lactose Operon.* Cold Spring Harbor, N.Y.: Cold Spring Harbor Laboratory, 1970.

Russell, Peter. *Genetics.* Boston, Mass.: Scott, Foresman, 1995.

Johnson, George B. *How Scientists Think.* Dubuque, Iowa: Wm C. Brown, 1996.

Collaboration with Monod

In 1958 Jacob began a second highly successful collaboration, this time with Jacques Lucien Monod and Arthur Pardee, on the control of bacterial enzyme production. They discovered and described messenger RNA (mRNA), a biological macromolecule that carries genetic information from the deoxyribonucleic acid (DNA) to the ribosomes, where proteins are synthesized. Jacob and Monod were also the first to distinguish structural genes from regulatory genes. Structural genes encode proteins that are important for normal cellular activities, while the products of regulatory genes interact with the structural genes to inhibit or stimulate their expression.

The highlight of the Jacob and Monod collaboration came in 1960 with their proposal of the operon model for the regulation of genes in bacteria. This model made an immediate and profound impact on the science of molecular biology, and they shared the Nobel Prize in Physiology or Medicine for this work a mere five years later, in 1965.

Collaboration with Wollman

Jacob renewed his association with Élie Wollman in 1960, and, the following year, they published what has become a classic text in bacterial genetics: *La Sexualité des bacteries,* 1959 (*Sexuality and the Genetics of Bacteria,* 1961). Their discovery and description of episomes (stable, autonomous, nonchromosomal pieces of DNA) in bacteria had widespread applications. Such elements were later found in corn and fruit flies and have been of critical importance in cancer research.

The single most useful technique for mapping bacterial genes was also devised by Jacob and Wollman. Known as the interrupted mating procedure, it allows for the determination of precise map distances between closely linked genes. This genetic approach established the circularity of the bacterial genome.

Philosophy of Science

Jacob made an abrupt shift in the 1970s to study embryology and development in mice. In particular, he studied teratocarcinoma, a type of germ cell tumor, as a system to investigate early developmental processes in mammals.

In addition, Jacob made excursions into scientific philosophy, resulting in the writing of two well-known works, *La Logique du vivant* (1970; *The Logic of Life*, 1973) and *Le Jeu des possibles* (1981; *The Possible and the Actual*, 1982). *La Statue intérieure*, published in 1987 and translated as *The Statue Within* (1988), is an autobiographical account that also focuses heavily on Jacob's philosophy of science.

Bibliography

By Jacob

Les Bactéries lysogènes et la notion de provirus, 1954.

La Sexualité des bactéries, 1959 (with Élie L. Wollman; *Sexuality and the Genetics of Bacteria*, 1961).

La Logique du vivant: une histoire de l'hérédité, 1970 (*The Logic of Life: A History of Heredity*, 1973).

Le Jeu des possibles: essai sur la diversité de vivant, 1981 (*The Possible and the Actual*, 1982).

La Statue intérieure, 1987 (*The Statue Within: An Autobiography*, 1988).

About Jacob

Nobel Lectures in Molecular Biology, 1933-1975. New York: Elsevier, 1977.

Judson, Horace F. *The Eighth Day of Creation: Makers of the Revolution in Biology.* New York: Simon & Schuster, 1979.

Harré, Rom. *Great Scientific Experiments: Twenty Experiments That Changed Our View of the World.* New York: Oxford University Press, 1983.

"François Jacob – Biographical," Nobelprize.org, //http: www.nobelprize.org/nobel_prizes/medicine/laureates/1965/jacob-bio.html

Yardley, William, "François Jacob, Geneticist Who Pointed to How Traits Are Inherited, Dies at 92," *New York Times*, April 25, 2013, http://www.nytimes.com/2013/04/26/science/francois-jacob-geneticist-who-pointed-to-how-traits-are-inherited-dies-at-92.html

(Jeffrey A. Knight)

Edward Jenner

Disciplines: Immunology and medicine
Contribution: Jenner, a country doctor, invented the method of disease prevention known as vaccination and helped to eradicate smallpox. His work inspired the creation of the branch of science called immunology.

May 17, 1749	Born in Berkeley, Gloucestershire, England
1770	Studies medicine at St. George's Hospital in London
1771	Prepares specimens from Captain Cook's first Pacific voyage
1772	Declines to serve as a naturalist on Cook's second expedition
1788	Fellow of the Royal Society of London
1792	Receives an M.D. from St. Andrew's Hospital
1796	Inoculates a boy with cowpox and confirms his subsequent immunity to smallpox
1798	Publishes his findings regarding inoculation
1802	Awarded £30,000 by Parliament for his dedication and achievements
1803	Founds the Royal Jennerian Society, which closes in 1806 and is replaced by the National Vaccine Establishment in 1808
1813	Presented with a Doctor in Physic degree by Oxford University 1815
1820	Suffers a stroke
Jan. 26, 1823	Dies in Berkeley, Gloucestershire, England

Early Life

Edward Jenner was born in the village of Berkeley in Gloucestershire, England, on May 17, 1749. His father, Reverend Steven Jenner, the vicar of Berkeley, died when Edward was only five years old. Edward attended local schools administrated by the clergy and developed an affinity for natural history and nature.

Jenner was apprenticed to Daniel Ludlow in Sodbury, located just outside of Bristol. During his apprenticeship, Jenner's interest in smallpox was sparked by a milkmaid's assertion that because she had contracted cowpox, she could not contract smallpox. In 1770 Jenner left Berkeley to study medicine at St. George's Hospital in London, where he lived with, and studied under, the anatomist John Hunter for two years.

Dr. Jenner Conquers Smallpox

In 1780 Jenner began research and experimentation on smallpox. In 1788 while involved in smallpox

The Development of the Smallpox Vaccine

Jenner discovered that inoculating humans with the milder cowpox or grease strains of the smallpox virus renders them immune to it..

Jenner believed that cowpox (in cows), the grease (in horses), and smallpox (in humans) were caused by the same "distemper," or infectious matter. He based his theory on evidence provided by milkmaids, who claimed that they could not contract smallpox. Jenner established the connection between the grease and cowpox by placing matter from the hoof of an infected horse on the udder of a cow, causing it to contract cowpox. Jenner then used pus from sores caused by the diseases to obtain vaccines and tested his method.

Inoculation was more successful than other methods of disease prevention at the time, but Jenner noted a disturbing number of failed vaccinations performed by other physicians. He found that the vaccine was effective only if certain conditions were met: it must be administered through the skin on the eighth day of the disease, and the pustular matter used in the vaccine must be stored properly.

Another cause of ineffective vaccinations was the inoculation of patients with matter from a "spurious cowpox" disease. Cows frequently were stricken with another disease with symptoms similar to those of "true" cowpox. Jenner delineated the difference between the two diseases to help eliminate impotent vaccines.

Jenner's vaccine was key in the eradication of smallpox from human populations. His method of vaccination led to major advances in the control and prevention of other diseases.

Bibliography

Jenner, Edward. *An Inquiry into the Causes and Effects of the Variolæ-Vaccinæ.* London: Sampson Low, 1789.

Jenner, Edward. *Further Observations on the Variolæ-Vaccinæ, or Cow Pox.* London: Sampson Low, 1799.

Chase, Allan. *Magic Shots: A Human and Scientific Account of the Long and Continuing Struggle to Eradicate Infectious Diseases by Vaccination.* New York: William Morrow, 1982.

research, Jenner married Catherine Kingscote. Together, the couple lived in a house called "The Chantry," which was their permanent residence for the rest of their lives. The couple produced two sons.

In 1792 Jenner received his doctor of medicine certification and began his medical practice in Gloucestershire. Despite the rigors of rural medical practice, he continued his work with smallpox and, in 1796, successfully inoculated eight-year-old James Phipps, using cowpox. He submitted the results and details of his experiment to the Royal Society of London. In response, the society deemed that a single, isolated success was inconclusive.

In 1798 after collecting twenty-three additional case histories to support his original experiment, Jenner published the pamphlet *An Inquiry into the Causes and Effects of the Variolæ-Vaccinæ, a Disease Discovered in Some of the Western Counties of England, Particularly Gloucestershire, and Known by the Name of the Cow Pox.* Interest in Jenner's work was sparked not only within the medical profession but also among laypeople throughout the world.

In 1802 Parliament received a petition to reimburse Jenner for the loss of income caused by his work on the smallpox vaccine. Jenner was against the proposal, but Parliament nevertheless granted him a total of £30,000.

Jenner's Work Continues

The next year, Jenner helped to found the Royal Jennerian Society. The society provided free vaccinations and a facility to collect the lymph fluid necessary to produce the vaccine. After the society was founded, the average number of deaths from smallpox in England dropped from 2,018 to 622 a year. The Royal Jennerian Society closed in 1806 as a result of management problems, but within two years it was replaced by the National Vaccine Establishment.

Jenner was continually contacted personally by people from around the world wishing to know more about his vaccine and the lymph needed to administer it. The deluge of requests spurred Jenner to call himself the "Vaccine Clerk to the World."

In 1815 Jenner's wife died, prompting his retirement. He became ill shortly thereafter and died following a stroke (commonly called a "fit of apoplexy") on January 26, 1823. He was buried in the parish church in Berkeley.

Bibliography

By Jenner

An Inquiry into the Causes and Effects of the Variolæ-Vaccinæ, a Disease Discovered in Some of the Western Counties of England, Particularly Gloucestershire, and Known by the Name of the Cow Pox, 1798.

Further Observations on the Variolæ-Vaccinæ, or Cow Pox, 1799.

About Jenner

Barron, John. *The Fife of Edward Jenner*. London: Henry Colburn, 1827.

Walker, M. E. M. *Pioneers of Public Health: The Story of Some Benefactors of the Human Race*. Edinburgh, Scotland: Oliver & Boyd, 1930.

(Alvin M. Pettus)

Shibasaburo Kitasato

Disciplines: Bacteriology and immunology
Contribution: A pioneering bacteriologist, Kitasato conducted investigations into tetanus and diphtheria that opened the new discipline of serology, which became immunology.

Dec. 20, 1852	Born in Oguni, Kumamoto, Japan
1872	Enrolls at the Kumamoto Medical Academy and comes under the influence of Dutch physician C. G. van Mansveldt
1883	Graduated from Tokyo University with a medical degree and joins the Public Health Bureau of Japan
1886	Travels to Germany for advanced training with Robert Koch in Berlin
1889	Produces the first pure culture of *Clostridium tetani*
1890	With Emil Adolf von Behring, publishes a paper on immunity to diphtheria and tetanus
1892	Returns to Japan and helps establish the Institute for Infectious Diseases
1894	Studies the outbreak of bubonic plague in Hong Kong
1899-1914	Director of the Institute of Infectious Diseases
1914	Establishes the Kitasato Institute for microbiological research
1917	First dean of the school of medicine at Keio University, Tokyo
1925	Elected the first president of the Japanese Medical Association
June 13, 1931	Dies in Nakanojo, Gumma, Japan

Early Life

Shibasaburo Kitasato (pronounced "kee-tah-Zah-toh") was the eldest son of Korenobu Kitasato, the mayor of the Oguni village in Kumamoto prefecture, in the southern island of Kyushu in Japan. The location of Kitasato's birthplace was a major influence on his future career as a medical microbiologist. In the mid-nineteenth century, before the Meiji Restoration, native Japanese people had limited access to foreign educational influence except in Nagasaki, a city also located on Kyushu, where Dutch intellectuals were allowed to teach and practice medicine.

In his early years Kitasato was not much interested in book learning, and his parents thought that he would become a farmer. According to Kitasato scholar James R. Bartholomew, however, three physicians influenced him: "his great-uncle, Hashimoto Ryu'un, a teacher named Tanaka Shiba, and a Dutch navy doctor C. G. van Mansveldt." At the age of nineteen, Kitasato entered Kumamoto

Medical Academy and came under the strong influence of Mansveldt for three years.

From Mansveldt, the young Kitasato learned about medicine, the German language, and Western culture, and was introduced to bacteria through microscopy. His mentor advised Kitasato to continue his studies at Tokyo University and then proceed to Germany. He was graduated from Tokyo in 1883 with a medical degree and then joined the newly established Public Health Bureau of Japan as a government medical officer. In the following year, Kitasato married Torako Matsuo.

Koch's Protégé

In 1886 Kitasato, sponsored by the Public Health Bureau, traveled to Berlin, Germany, to train with Robert Koch, the most renowned bacteriologist of his era. Before he returned to Japan in 1892, Kitasato had established a reputation as an eminent researcher in bacteriology by publishing papers that later came to be acknowledged as classics. The year 1889 turned out to be a peak in Kitasato's productivity. He published a total of fifteen papers, among which two were of significance. In one paper, he established that a bacillus bacterium, *Clostridium tetani*, causes tetanus. In another paper, he described a method of culturing anaerobic C. *chauvoei*, the causative agent of the blackleg disease in cattle.

In 1889 Emil Adolf von Behring, an army physician, joined Koch's research team. Kitasato collaborated with Behring to develop a strategy for protection against diphtheria (one of the lethal diseases to which children often succumbed) and tetanus. A year later, they co-authored a paper entitled "Über das Zustandekommen der Diphtherie-Immunität und der Tetanus-Immunität bei Thieren" (the mechanism of immunity in animals to diphtheria and tetanus), which appeared in *Deutsche Medizinische Wochenschrift*. This paper is now acknowledged as one of the foundation stones of the discipline of immunology.

A Dispute About Bubonic Plague

Kitasato returned to Japan in 1892, and, when an outbreak of bubonic plague occurred in Hong Kong two years later, he was sent there by the Japanese government. He accepted the challenge of identifying the causative pathogen of the plague. Alexandre Yersin, a Swiss-born medical doctor, also arrived in Hong Kong from the then-French colony of Indochina (now Vietnam).

In the ensuing competition between these scientists, Kitasato described his pathogen as a gram-positive bacillus, *Pasteurella pestis*, while Yersin found the bacillus to be gram-negative (according to a test called Gram staining). Later investigations showed that Yersin had described the true causative organism of the plague and that Kitasato might have mistaken a contaminant as the causative pathogen.

An Institution Builder

Apart from being a reputed scientist, Kitasato also invested much of his time in building scientific institutions in the then-developing Japan. He played a role in establishing the Institute of Infectious Diseases in Tokyo and served as its director from 1899 to 1914. His notable protégés included Kiyoshi Shiga, who identified the pathogen of dysentery, and Sahachiro Hata, who gained recognition as bacteriologist Paul Ehrlich's associate in the discovery of the antisyphilitic drug Salvarsan.

In 1914 Kitasato set up his private Kitasato Institute for research in microbiology, and in 1923

The Demonstration of Passive Immunity

Immunity acquired by an individual from a passive transfer—such as the immunity of newborns resulting from the transfer of antibodies in the ingestion of colostrum in mother's milk or the immunity that results from the administration of antitoxins or antivenoms—is known as passive immunity.

The phenomenon of passive immunity was described by Emil Adolf von Behring and Kitasato in their classic 1890 paper. They immunized rabbits against a culture containing virulent tetanus bacilli. Then, they collected blood from the carotid artery of the rabbits and injected 0.2 to 0.5 milliliter of serum (blood fluid before coagulation) into the abdominal cavity of mice. They inoculated the mice with virulent tetanus bacilli and observed the effect of immunity after twenty-four hours.

Behring and Kitasato made the following inferences from their observations. First, the blood of rabbits immune to tetanus had the ability to neutralize or destroy the tetanus toxin. Second, this property existed also in extravascular blood and in cell-free serum. Third, this property is so stable that it remained effective even in the body of other animals. Thus, through blood or serum transformations, one can achieve outstanding therapeutic effects.

The paper by Behring and Kitasato presented the first evidence that some substances produced in the serum in response to infection are able to neutralize foreign materials. The term "antitoxin" was first introduced in this paper, in its German variant as "antitoxisch."

This discovery opened the possibility of specific therapy for diseases through the injection of immune serum. Kitasato is recognized for his experimental rigor and exploratory skills in demonstrating the immunological phenomenon of passive immunity.

Bibliography

Magill, Frank N, ed. "Behring Discovers the Diphtheria Antitoxin," *Great Events from History II: Science and Technology Series*. Pasadena, Calif.: Salem Press, 1991.

Kantha, Sachi Sri. "A Centennial Review: The 1890 Tetanus Antitoxin Paper of von Behring and Kitasato and the Related Developments," *Keio Journal of Medicine* 40 (1991; Japan).

he was elected as the first president of the Japanese Medical Association. After a productive five-decade career in research and science administration, Kitasato died of a stroke in Japan at the age of seventy-nine.

Medical historians now believe that Kitasato was unfortunate in not being named a joint winner of the first Nobel Prize in Physiology or Medicine, in 1901, which was awarded solely to Behring for the discovery of natural immunity. Kitasato made substantial contributions to the research described in the 1890 paper on natural immunity that he coauthored with Behring.

Bibliography

By Kitasato

"Über den Tetanuserreger," *Deutsche Medizinische Wochenschrift*, 1889.

"Über den Rauschbrandbacillus und sein Culturfahren," *Zeitschrift für Hygiene und Infektionskrankheiten*, 1889.

"Über das Zustandekommen der Diphtherie-Immunität und der Tetanus-Immunität bei Thieren," *Deutsche Medizinische Wochenschrift*, 1890 (with Emil Adolf von Behring).

"Heilversuchean tetanuskranken Thieren," *Zeitschrift für Hygiene und Infektionskrankheiten*, 1892.

Baikingaku Kenkyu, 1893.

"The Bacillus of Bubonic Plague," *The Lancet*, 1894.

About Kitasato

Fox, H. "Baron Shibasaburo Kitasato," *Annals of Medical History*, 6 (1934).

Gillispie, Charles Coulston, ed. *Dictionary of Scientific Biography*. Vol. 7. New York: Charles Scribner's Sons, 1973.

Bibel, David J. and T. H. Chen. "Diagnosis of Plague: An Analysis of the Yersin-Kitasato Controversy." *Bacteriological Reviews* 40 (September, 1976).

Bartholomew, James R. *The Formation of Science in Japan: Building a Research Tradition*. New Haven, Conn.: Yale University Press, 1989.

Bendiner, Jessica and Elmer Bendiner. *Biographical Dictionary of Medicine*. New York: Facts on File, 1990.

(Sachi Sri Kantha)

Robert Koch

Disciplines: Bacteriology and medicine

Contribution: Koch isolated the etiological agents for a variety of infectious diseases, including anthrax, tuberculosis, and cholera.

Dec. 11, 1843	Born in Clausthal, Prussia (now Germany)
1866	Earns a medical degree at the University of Göttingen
1866	Medical assistant at Hamburg General Hospital
1870-1871	Physician with the German army during the Franco-Prussian War
1873-1876	Conducts research on anthrax, resulting in the isolation of the etiological agent
1880	Staff member of the Imperial Health Office in Berlin
1881-1882	Studies tuberculosis, isolating the causative bacillus
1883	Formulates what has become known as Koch's postulates
1883-1884	Conducts research on cholera, culminating in the isolation of the etiological agent
1885	Professor of Hygiene at the University of Berlin
1890	Announces a tuberculosis cure that is later proved incorrect
1900	The Robert Koch Institute for Infectious Diseases opens in Berlin
1905	Awarded the Nobel Prize in Physiology or Medicine
May 27, 1910	Dies in Baden-Baden, Germany

Early Life

Heinrich Hermann Robert Koch (pronounced "kawk") was born in 1843 in the small mining town of Clausthal, Prussia, as the third of thirteen children. The strongest influence in his life, relevant to his later pursuits, was his uncle, Eduard Biewend, who strongly encouraged Koch's interests in both nature and photography. Koch entered the gymnasium in 1851, at the age of eight, and demonstrated a strong aptitude for both mathematics and the sciences.

Koch's interest in a university education, particularly one in science, resulted in his enrollment in the University of Göttingen in 1862. While there, he won a prize of thirty ducats for his anatomical study of the nerve distribution in uterine ganglia. Koch used his prize money to attend a professional meeting in Hanover, where he had the opportunity to meet some of the most renowned scientists in Germany. This study, which resulted in his first professional publication, also

Isolation of the Tuberculosis Bacillus

During the nineteenth century, tuberculosis was the deadliest respiratory disease in the world; one-seventh of all deaths were caused by this disease. Koch's isolation of the etiological (causative) agent established the infectious nature of the disease.

In his earlier research, Koch had developed principles of photomicroscopy and bacterial culture in the study of microorganisms. He was able to apply these principles to the isolation of the tuberculosis bacillus and the demonstration of its role in the disease.

Koch began his first experiment on the problem on August 18, 1881. Other scientists had attempted to isolate the organism; indeed, as a specific disease, tuberculosis had been known for thousands of years. Such attempts were never successful, however, and the causative agent had never even been observed in tissue.

In this respect, Koch brought a unique quality to the research: patience. Many scientists had been at work on the problem, but repeated negative results had frustrated them. Koch was convinced that the organism was there. What was required was the discovery of appropriate techniques for its study.

His initial experiments dealt with developing a method to observe the organism. Through intense work, he found that a procedure using an alkaline dye was successful in staining the microbe; he was thus able to observe rod-shaped organisms in the lung tissue from patients with tuberculosis. This work proved to be the most important step in establishing the cause of the disease.

The application of what have become known as Koch's postulates confirmed the role of these microbes as the cause of tuberculosis. Koch was able to observe large numbers of these organisms in all infected tissue; if the nature of the disease improved and the patient recovered, fewer organisms were observed.

To establish firmly the role played by these bacteria, however, it would be necessary to culture (grow) them in the laboratory and to demonstrate that pure cultures could be used to transmit the disease—again, an aspect of the postulates. Koch found that the organism had strict nutritional requirements and would only grow in a special medium containing coagulated blood. Nevertheless, he was able to grow the organism; guinea pigs inoculated with the cultures became ill.

Koch announced the results of the study at a lecture to the Berlin Physiological Society on March 24, 1882. Not only did he report the work, he also brought an extensive array of material to demonstrate his methodology: test tubes with cultures, a microscope, chemicals for staining, and photographs. When Koch published the results of his work some weeks later in the journal *Berliner Klinischen Wochenschrift*, it created intense excitement throughout both the general population and the scientific world.

Bibliography

Bulloch, William. *A History of Bacteriology*. London: Oxford University Press, 1938.

Dubos, René and Jean Dubos. *The White Plague*. Boston: Little, Brown, 1956.

Ryan, Frank. *The Forgotten Plague*. Boston: Little, Brown, 1994.

became the basis for his doctoral dissertation. At the age of twenty-three, Koch was graduated with a doctoral degree from the university.

Interests in Research

Following his graduation, and engaged to marry, Koch accepted a position at the Hamburg General Hospital. It was there that he developed his first interests in research. Unable to support a family on his salary at the hospital, however, Koch resigned in favor of a position in Langenhagen, in an institution for the care and education of special needs children. Koch remained there two years.

Koch spent several years in medical practice in a variety of towns. Eventually, he settled in Rakwitz, where his medical skills became well known. In 1870 the Franco-Prussian War intervened. Koch spent two years serving as a physician with the German forces. Following his discharge, he was accepted for the position of *Kreisphysikus*, or district medical officer, in the city of Wöllstein.

In Wöllstein, Koch began his study of anthrax. Although bacilli had already been observed in the blood of sick animals, their role in the disease remained uncertain. In 1873 Koch began his research on the illness by repeating the microscopic observations of others.

While studying bacterial cultures isolated from the blood of animals with anthrax, Koch observed that these bacteria form spores, a dormant stage that allows them to survive. He also demonstrated that pure cultures of these bacteria can be used to infect test animals, causing development of the disease. This work later formed the basis for what became known as Koch's postulates—a means of associating disease with specific bacterial agents.

Isolation of the Tuberculosis Bacillus

In 1880 Koch moved to Berlin as a staff member of the Imperial Health Office. There, he applied his earlier research on microscopy and microbial isolation to the problem of tuberculosis.

Koch began his work on the isolation of the tuberculosis bacillus in August, 1881. Using a variety of staining techniques, he was able to demonstrate the presence of the bacterium within infected lung tissue. He was also able to culture the organism in the laboratory and to demonstrate that pure cultures of the bacilli could cause the same disease in guinea pigs.

Koch reported his results to the Berlin Physiological Society in March, 1882, only seven months after beginning his work.

Isolation of the Cholera Bacillus

In 1883 Koch was appointed head of the German Cholera Commission, which was sent to Egypt to investigate the outbreak of an epidemic of cholera. By the time that the commission reached Egypt, the epidemic had already begun to wane. Consequently, Koch followed the outbreak to India, where he was able to isolate and grow the agent that causes the disease.

Koch returned to Germany in 1884. He was greeted as a hero and eventually became the head of his own institute.

The Final Years

Koch again turned his research to the problem of tuberculosis. He became obsessed with the idea that inactivation of the causative bacillus could be used as the basis for a tuberculosis vaccine (tuberculin). Unfortunately, the idea proved invalid and so discredited some of his work.

Despite some failures, Koch was recognized in his later years as perhaps the greatest pure bacteriologist in the world. In addition to his isolation of the bacilli that cause several of the most important infectious diseases, Koch's culture methods and development of photomicroscopy revolutionized science.

In 1905 Koch was awarded the Nobel Prize in Physiology or Medicine for his work, ostensibly for isolation of the tuberculosis bacillus but in reality to honor a man who had done so much. In 1910 Koch died from a sudden heart attack.

Bibliography

By Koch

"Über das Vorkommen von Ganglienzellen an den Nerven des Uterus," 1865.

"Die Ätiologie der Milzbrand-Krankheit, begründet auf die Entwicklungsgeschichte des Bacillus Anthracis," *Beiträge zur Biologie der Pflanzen*, 1876 ("The Etiology of Anthrax Based on the Life History of *Bacillus anthracis*," *Milestones in Microbiology*, 1961).

"Verfahren zur Untersuchung, zum Konservieren und Photographiren der Bakterien," *Beiträge zur Biologie der Pflanzen*, 1877.

Untersuchungen über die Aetiologie der Wundinfectionskrankheiten, 1878 (*Investigations into the Etiology of Traumatic Infective Diseases*, 1880).

"Zur Untersuchung von pathogenen Organismen," *Mittheilungen aus dem kaiserlichen Gesundheitsamte*, 1881 ("Methods for the Study of Pathogenic Organisms," *Milestones in Microbiology*, 1961).

"Die Ätiologie der Tuberkulose," *Berliner Klinischen Wochenschrift*, 1882 ("The Etiology of Tuberculosis—Koch's Postulates," *Milestones in Microbiology*, 1961).

"Über die Cholerabakterien," *Deutsche Medizinische Wochenschrift*, 1884.

"Fortsetzung der Mittheilungen über ein Heilmittel gegen Tuberkulose," *Deutsche Medizinische Wochenschrift*, 1891.

"Erste Bericht über die Tätigkeit der Malariaexpedition," *Deutsche Medizinische Wochenschrift*, 1899.

About Koch

De Kruif, Paul. *Microbe Hunters*. New York: Harcourt, Brace & World, 1953.

Baldry, Peter. *The Battle Against Bacteria*, Cambridge, England: Cambridge University Press, 1976.

Brock, Thomas D. *Robert Koch: A Life in Medicine and Bacteriology*. New York: Springer-Verlag, 1988.

Fisher, Linda. "Robert Koch," *The Nobel Prize Winners: Physiology or Medicine*. Frank N. Magill, ed. Pasadena, Calif.: Salem Press, 1991.

(Richard Adler)

Alphonse Laveran

Disciplines: Medicine, pharmacology, and zoology

Contribution: Laveran was the first to demonstrate that protozoa can cause disease. His work with malaria won for him the Nobel Prize in Physiology or Medicine in 1907.

June 18, 1845	Born in Paris, France
1867	Graduated from the École du Service de Santé Militaire in Strasbourg
1878-1883	Serves in Algeria and begins his studies into the cause of malaria
1879	Publishes a two-volume work on pathology and clinical medicine
Nov. 6, 1880	Makes a critical observation of a malaria parasite
1884	Publishes a treatise on palustral fevers
1889	Receives the Bréant Prize from the Académie des Sciences
1896	Joins the Institut Pasteur
1901	Elected a member of the Académie des Sciences
1904	Publishes *Trypanosomes et trypanosomiases (Trypanosomes and Trypanosomiases,* 1907)
1907	Receives the Nobel Prize in Physiology or Medicine
1912	Made a commander in the Legion of Honor
May 18, 1922	Dies in Paris, France

Early Life

Charles Louis Alphonse Laveran (pronounced "la-VRAHN") was born in Paris in 1845. Several members of his family were physicians or military officers, a heritage that he continued in his career.

When Laveran was only five, his family moved to Algeria, where he was taught mostly by his father. After returning to Paris, he completed his secondary education at the Lycée Louis-le-Grand and studied medicine in Strasbourg. In 1874 by taking a competitive examination, he earned the chair formerly held by his father at the Val-de-Grâce military academy in Paris.

Army Life and Opportunity

The French army never noticed Laveran's talent for research, and he was frequently sent to posts with extensive administrative duties and no research opportunities. It is a tribute to his character that he would not allow these circumstances to nullify his gifts. During a potentially wasted assignment

Protozoa as Medical Parasites

It was common knowledge at the end of the nineteenth century that disease was caused by bacteria. But Laveran's discovery of a protozoan in the blood as the cause of malaria came as a great surprise to the medical world.

After Louis Pasteur proved his germ theory of disease, people believed that bacteria were the ultimate disease-causing organisms. Two Italian scientists published research claiming that a specific bacterium, *Bacillus malariae*, found in the soil and water of fever-infested areas, caused malaria.

Blood from the corpse of a fever victim shows a black pigment, or melanemia. When blood is taken from the liver capillaries of a living malaria patient, the red blood cells have pigmented bodies with distinctive shapes and color. The patient's white blood cells also contain the black pigment, and outside the blood cells are crescent and spherical bodies with black fragments.

A critical observation of the malaria protozoa can be made when a blood sample is taken from a patient during a fever attack. In addition to the crescent-shaped bodies, those cells having a spherical shape show a series of fine, transparent filaments. These flagella, which are characteristic of the one-celled animals called protozoa, move actively among the red blood cells. Some of the flagella separate and disappear; these represent the male component in the sexual reproduction of protozoa.

Bibliography

Curtis, Helena. *The Marvelous Animals: An Introduction to the Protozoa*. New York: Natural History Press, 1968.

Schmidt, Gerald D. and Donald A. Klein. *Foundations of Parasitology*. 2d ed. St. Louis, Mo.: C. V. Mosby, 1981.

Prescott, Lansing M., John P. Harley, and Donald A. Klein. *Microbiology*. Dubuque, Iowa: Wm. C. Brown, 1990.

in Algeria, he carried out his most important work, the identification of the cause of malaria.

The comparison of fresh blood from both healthy and afflicted soldiers led to his hypothesis that a protozoan offered the best explanation of the known facts about the disease. The accepted idea that bacteria were the cause of malaria, however, led most medical workers to insist that water, air, or soil must contain a causative bacterium. Laveran's work was disregarded for four years.

Ultimately, the weight of evidence became overpowering, and his research gained nearly universal acceptance. During this period, he had continued active research on the subject but had been unable to work out the full development of the parasite's life cycle. The problem was complicated: in Algeria, there are three separate, and common, forms of malaria. Laveran published his opinion that the mosquito is responsible for the life of the parasite outside the human body.

Working in India, Sir Ronald Ross later proved that the *Anopheles* mosquito is the required host for malaria. When he won the 1902 Nobel Prize in Physiology or Medicine, Ross gave Laveran credit for putting him on the right track.

Enough of the Army—But Not of the Protozoa

Even though his work won general acceptance, the army refused to provide for the development of Laveran's skills. Reluctantly, despite the pleas of fellow officers, he resigned his commission in 1896 and joined the Institut Pasteur in Paris. There, in the company of able colleagues, he found an environment in which he could grow; he intensified and expanded his studies of protozoa and disease.

Over the next twenty years, Laveran continued to make important studies of these tiny creatures. He made contributions to the eventual identification of the parasite that causes sleeping sickness. In other studies of tropical fevers, he greatly advanced the techniques required for the laboratory study of protozoa.

It is a curious fact that the Nobel Prize must be given for "recent work." Thus, Laveran technically received this belated recognition for his work "on the role played by protozoa in causing disease," not for his discovery concerning malaria.

Laveran was made a commander in the Legion of Honor in 1912. He died in 1922 at the age of seventy-six.

Bibliography

By Laveran

Nouveaux éléments de pathologie et de clinique médicales, 1879 (2 vols.; with J. Teissier).

"Un nouveau parasite trouvé dans le sang des maladies atteints de fièvre palustre," *Bulletin de Mémoriale Société de Médicale Hôpital de Paris,* 1880 (a new parasite found in the blood of those sick with palustrial fever).

Traité des fièvres palustres: avec la description des microbes du paludisme, 1884 (*Traits of Palustrial Fever with a Description of the Palustrial Microbes,* 1884).

Trypanosomes et trypanosomiases, 1904 (with F. Mesnil; *Trypanosomes and Trypanosomiases,* 1907).

About Laveran

Klein, Marc. *"Laveran, Charles Louis Alphonse," Dictionary of Scientific Biography.* New York: Charles Scribner's Sons, 1973.

Lambert, Lisa A. "Alphonse Laveran," *The Nobel Prize Winners: Physiology or Medicine.* Frank N. Magill, ed. Pasadena, Calif.: Salem Press, 1991.

(K. Thomas Finley)

Antoni van Leeuwenhoek

Disciplines: Bacteriology, biology, cell biology, and medicine

Contribution: As the first microscopist to create powerful lenses, Leeuwenhoek made many discoveries concerning the description and reproduction of bacteria, protozoa, plants, and animals.

Oct. 24, 1632	Born in Delft, the Netherlands
1650	Becomes a shopkeeper
1660	Becomes a civil servant
1665	Constructs his first microscopes
1668	Develops the theory of blood circulation through capillaries
1674	Describes red blood corpuscles
1675	Describes microorganisms, including bacteria and protozoa, which he termed "animalicules"
1677	Describes animal sperm and eggs and provides evidence against the theory of spontaneous generation
1680	Fellow of the Royal Society of London
1685	Investigates plant reproduction
1699	Appointed as a correspondent of the Académie des Sciences in Paris
1716	Awarded a silver medal by the Louvain College of Professors
Aug. 26, 1723	Dies in Delft, the Netherlands

Early Life

Antoni van Leeuwenhoek (pronounced "LAY-vehn-hewk") was born in Delft, the son of a middle-class basket maker who died when Antoni was six years old. Leeuwenhoek attended grammar school in a village near Leiden, the Netherlands, but never received a university education and instead went to Amsterdam to apprentice himself to a cloth merchant. After setting up a shop in Delft and marrying his first wife, he accepted a civil post in Delft, serving the city in various capacities. After the death of his first wife, he remarried, but the death of his second wife preceded his own by almost thirty years.

Leeuwenhoek's scientific career began as a hobby. He gained mathematical skills, which were necessary for his duties as a civil servant, and he taught himself to make tiny magnifying lenses, initially for the purpose of inspecting the quality of cloth. He ground these lenses by hand from glass globules. He had excellent vision, mathematical exactitude, tremendous manual dexterity, and patience—all of which contributed to his success.

The Microscope

With these lenses, Leeuwenhoek constructed microscopes with magnifying powers of up to 500 times normal viewing power. These devices allowed him to visualize objects with a diameter of about 1 micron. His art, however, died with him. Microscopes equivalent to those that he made did not become available until the advent of the compound microscope in the nineteenth century.

Leeuwenhoek's scientific activities first began when he was almost forty years old. Because of his meager education, he knew only one language, Dutch, and could not communicate with foreign scientists. He worked in near isolation, seldom leaving the Netherlands. He wrote nearly 200 letters to the Royal Society of London, his primary scientific contact, but these had to be translated.

Initially, Leeuwenhoek's observations were questioned, and scientists traveled great distances to Delft to confirm his reports, which caused quite a furor in the Royal Society of London. He was the first person to describe eukaryotic microorganisms, as well as the three principal shapes of bacteria (spherical, rod-shaped, and spiral-shaped), though he erroneously thought of microorganisms as little animals and called them "animalicules." Leeuwenhoek observed sperm and egg cells from many different species, argued against the then-prevalent theory of spontaneous generation, and set the groundwork for the present understanding of fertilization. He also devoted much time to the characterization of blood circulation and muscle structure, thereby providing a basis for an understanding of animal physiology.

Leeuwenhoek's devotion to his studies led to worldwide recognition. His discoveries at the frontier of microscopy were followed with interest throughout England and Europe. He became so famous that many dignitaries, including kings and princes, visited him. Among these were Queen Anne of England, Peter the Great of Russia, and Frederick the Great of Prussia. Leeuwenhoek continued his work for nearly half a century until his death at the age of ninety.

Bibliography

By Leeuwenhoek

His collected Dutch edition, the *Brieven*, consists of four volumes.

Vol. 1: *Brieven, Geschreven aan de Wytvermaarde Koninglijke Wetenschapzoekende Societeit, tot Londen in Engeland*, 1684–1694 (10 parts; with a Register, 1695).

Vol. 2: *Vervolg Der Brieven, Geschreven aan de Wytvermaarde Koninglijke Societeit in Londen*, 1688; *Tweede Vervolg Der Brieven*, 1689; *Derde Vervolg Der Brieven*, 1693; and *Vierde Vervolg Der Brieven*, 1694.

Vol. 3: *Vijfde Vervolg Der Brieven, Geschreven*

A Modern Light Microscope

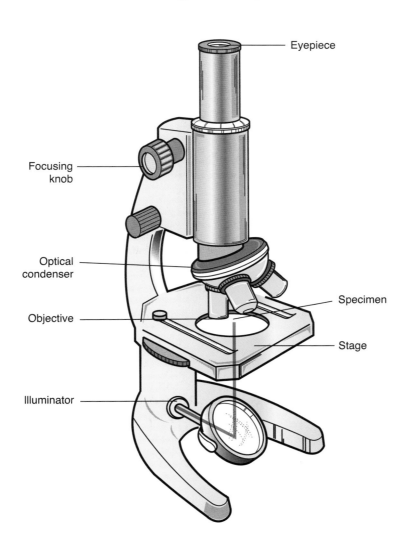

The First Microscopist

Leeuwenhoek can be considered the world's first microscopist. Although he also examined inanimate objects, almost all of his valued discoveries resulted from the description of living things, such as bacteria, yeast, ciliates, and many higher organisms, including humans.

Many of Leeuwenhoek's important discoveries opposed the then-prevalent theory of spontaneous generation. He showed that weevils and other insects did not derive from decaying organic matter. Instead, they arose from sperm and eggs, as do mammals. His studies set the stage for the modern view of fertilization as the unified basis for reproduction in all higher organisms.

In addition to his important advances in the study of animals and microbes, Leeuwenhoek described many important aspects of plants. He drew elaborate diagrams that led to an understanding of their physiological functions. He usually interpreted the structures that he observed correctly, in spite of (or maybe because of) his lack of familiarity with the scientific thought of his time.

Despite his numerous observational advances and his amazing interpretive insight, Leeuwenhoek missed some important concepts. For example, he never came to appreciate the cellular basis of life. Furthermore, in his description of microorganisms such as protozoa and bacteria, he always viewed them as miniature animals rather than as distinct life-forms. These deficiencies and misconceptions presumably reflected the time in which he lived. Modern thought has evolved gradually, as a result of continual change from established dogma.

Bibliography

De Kruif, Paul. *Microbe Hunters.* San Diego, Calif.: Harcourt, Brace, 1926.
Schierbeek, Abraham. *Measuring the Invisible World: The Life and Works of Antoni van Leeuwenhoek.* London: Abelard-Schuman, 1959.

aan verscheide Hoge Standspersonen en Geleerde Luijden, 1696; *Sesde Vervolg Der Brieven,* 1697; and *Sevende Vervolg Der Brieven,* 1702.
Vol. 4: *Send-Brieven,* 1718.
The Select Works of Antony van Leeuwenhoek, 1798-1807 (2 vols.; Samuel Hoole, ed.).
The Collected Letters of Antoni van Leeuwenhoek, 1939-1967 (8 vols.).
About Leeuwenhoek
Dobell, C. *Antony van Leeuwenhoek and His "Little Animals."* 2d ed. New York: 1958.
Schierbeek, Abraham. *Measuring the Invisible World: The Life and Works of Antoni van Leeuwenhoek.* London: Abelard-Schuman, 1959.

(Milton H. Saier, Jr.)

Joseph Lister

Disciplines: Bacteriology and medicine

Contribution: Lister developed the sterile procedures that resulted in antiseptic surgery. As one of the first scientists to grow bacteria in pure culture, he was also among the early pioneers of bacteriology.

Apr. 5, 1827	Born in Upton Park, Essex, England
1847-1852	Studies for a medical degree at University College, London
1853	Serves as house physician and surgeon at University College Hospital
1854	Studies under James Syme, professor of clinical surgery at Edinburgh
1855	Assistant surgeon to the Edinburgh Royal Infirmary
1860	Appointed to the Regius Chair of Surgery at Glasgow University
1860	Fellow of the Royal Society of London
1865	Tests his procedure of antiseptic surgery for the first time
1867	Publishes his works on antiseptic surgery in *The Lancet*
1869	Succeeds Syme in the Chair of Clinical Surgery at Edinburgh
1877-1892	Chair of Surgery at King's College, London
1895-1900	President of the Royal Society of London
1897	Elevated to the peerage as Joseph, Baron Lister
Feb. 10, 1912	Dies in Walmer, Kent, England

Early Life

Joseph Lister was born in a small village east of London in 1822. His father, Joseph Jackson Lister, was a wealthy wine merchant and a self-educated man versed in both mathematics and optics. The love of science was passed on to the younger Joseph, the second son in the household.

Lister showed an interest in nature at a young age and, after his early education in the Quaker school at Tottenham, enrolled at University College in London at the age of sixteen. In December, 1846, as a nineteen-year-old undergraduate student, he was present when Robert Liston, a professor of surgery at University College, carried out the first surgical operation under ether in Europe.

Following his graduation in 1847, Lister entered the medical program at University College. While still a student, he presented two papers, "Gangrene," and "Use of the Microscope in Medicine," in front of the Hospital Medical Society. Lister was graduated with honors in 1852.

Development of Aseptic Surgery

Lister determined that the source of infection during surgical procedures are microorganisms in the air. By maintaining sterile procedures, such wound contamination can be eliminated.

The prevailing theory concerning the source of surgical infection prior to Lister's time was addressed at oxygen in the air. It was believed that tissue became oxidized, breaking down and forming pus. Lister believed that the evidence made such a theory untenable, since tissue is routinely exposed to oxygen in the blood.

Louis Pasteur's discovery in the 1850s of the role played by microbes in putrefaction and fermentation provided the necessary answer for Lister: it is not the oxygen in the air that causes contamination, but microbes. Wound infection in humans was a counterpart to the contamination of beer and wine from microorganisms in the air. Lister thought that if such contamination could be prevented, the danger of wound sepsis would be reduced.

He was soon able to put his theory into practice. On August 12, 1865, Lister operated on a boy with a compound fracture of the tibia, with an exposed wound of several inches. After cleaning the wound, he applied a bandage soaked in carbolic acid. When fresh dressings were placed on the wound, they too were soaked in the solution. No infection developed.

Lister refined his technique in other operations. He began a thorough disinfection of the skin itself with carbolic acid. All instruments were likewise sterilized. Severe wounds with deep cavities were drained and the cavities washed and filled with the disinfectant solution. In addition, the surgeon's hands were thoroughly cleaned in the solution prior to the beginning of surgery.

The operating room itself was to be maintained in a condition as close to sterile as possible. For a time, a carbolic acid mist was sprayed in the air; this technique was unpopular and did not appear to be particularly effective anyway, and so it was stopped. Lister would not compromise, however, on the importance of sterile dressings and bandages. The preparations and procedures were complicated, but the results could not be disputed.

Lister published a complete summary of his work in an 1870 issue of the British journal *The Lancet*. The mortality rate associated with amputation had been reduced by two-thirds. The number of wounds that did not require amputation, since no infection developed, could not be calculated.

Although it was some years before Lister's practice of antiseptic surgery became universally accepted, it would eventually become a standard procedure. The danger of wound contamination will always remain, but such contamination during surgery is now the exception rather than a common problem.

Bibliography

Lechevalier, Hubert and Morris Solotorovsky. *Three Centuries of Microbiology*. New York: Dover, 1974.

Rains, A. H. *Joseph Lister and Antisepsis*. Hove, England: Priory Press, 1977.

Youngson, A. J. *The Scientific Revolution in Victorian Medicine*. New York: Holmes and Meier, 1979.

King, L. S. "Germ Theory and Its Influence," *Journal of the American Medical Association*, 249 (1983).

Medical Career

In 1852 Lister served a term as house physician, followed by nine months of service as a house surgeon. His interest in surgery as a career led Lister to move to Edinburgh in 1853, where he developed both a professional and a personal relationship with James Syme, one of the outstanding technical surgeons in Britain.

The outbreak of the Crimean War in 1855 led Lister to apply for a vacant position as staff surgeon at Edinburgh, and, in April, 1855, he was appointed assistant surgeon to the Edinburgh Royal Infirmary and lecturer in surgery to the Royal College of Surgeons. It was at this time that he began courting Syme's daughter, Agnes, whom he married in 1856.

Lister's reputation as both a teacher and a researcher continued to grow, and, when the position of professor of surgery at the University of Glasgow became available in 1859, he was recommended for the appointment. In 1860 he received the appointment to the Regius Chair of Surgery at Glasgow.

Antiseptic Surgery

With the introduction of general anesthesia to surgery in 1846, much of the reluctance on behalf of physicians to carry out surgical procedures disappeared. The numbers of practicing surgeons significantly increased, accompanied by a jump in the number of surgical procedures.

With surgery, however, came the danger of sepsis, or infection. Gangrene, often called "hospital fever," was a common occurrence, with the mortality associated with amputation as high as 60 percent in some hospitals. Rarely was any surgical procedure unaccompanied by infection. Most scientists believed that the cause was oxygen from the air.

In 1865 the French scientist Louis Pasteur had published his work on putrefaction and fermentation, associating each with microorganisms in the air. Pasteur's articles were read by Lister, who quickly realized their significance. Lister thought that by limiting contact of such organisms with the surgical incision, infection might be prevented.

On August 12, 1865, Lister attempted his first experiment in antiseptic surgery, operating on an eleven-year-old boy who had suffered a compound fracture. Following the surgery, Lister dressed the wound with bandages soaked in carbolic acid (phenol). All dressings were treated the same way, and no infection developed.

Over subsequent weeks, Lister continued to test his procedure of "carbolic acid antisepsis." The procedure was modified by treating the area around the incision with carbolic acid as well. Attempts to spray the air with carbolic acid proved less successful. By 1867, Lister was sufficiently satisfied with the procedure to publish his successful results in the British journal *The Lancet*.

Later Career

In 1869 an ailing Syme resigned his position at Edinburgh, and Lister was appointed his successor as chair of clinical surgery at the young age of forty-two.

It is ironic that despite the success of the antiseptic procedure and its acceptance in both France and Germany, Lister's techniques did not receive widespread recognition in England. In part, this was attributable to a reluctance to accept the germ theory of disease.

In 1877 Lister accepted an offer for the chair of surgery at the Medical School of King's College in London. It was his hope that antiseptic surgery would receive wider acceptance. Although his fellow surgeons would initially be hesitant to accept the truth of Lister's views on antisepsis, the results could not be ignored. Although infection remained a common occurrence in many surgical wards, rarely was it a problem when Lister's procedures were followed. By the 1880s, the acceptance of the germ theory was becoming universal.

Lister spent his last years researching a variety of subjects. He published work on inflammation and blood coagulation, and was among the first to grow microorganisms in pure culture for study. Lister became a baronet in 1883 and was made a peer in 1897. He continued to publish until well into his eightieth year and died in 1912.

Bibliography

By Lister

"Observations of the Contractile Tissue of the Iris," *Quarterly Journal of Microscopical Science*, 1853.

"Observations on the Muscular Tissue of the Skin," *Quarterly Journal of Microscopical Science*, 1853.

"Report of Some Cases of Maxillary Tumour," *Monthly Journal of Medical Science*, 1854.

"On the Early Stages of Inflammation," *Proceedings of the Royal Society*, 1857.

"Some Observations on the Structure of Nerve Fibres," *Quarterly Journal of Microscopical Science*, 1860 (with William Turner).

"On the Coagulation of the Blood," *Proceedings of the Royal Society*, 1863.

"On a New Method of Treating Compound Fracture, Abscess, etc., with Observations on the Conditions of Suppuration," *The Lancet* 1867.

"On the Antiseptic Principle in the Practice of Surgery," *The Lancet*, 1867.

"Observations in Ligature of Arteries on the Antiseptic System, *The Lancet*, 1869.

"Further Evidence Regarding the Effects of the Antiseptic Treatment upon the Salubrity of a Surgical Hospital," *The Lancet*, 1870.

"A Method of Antiseptic Treatment Applicable to Wounded Soldiers in the Present War," *British Medical Journal*, 1870.

"On the Relation of Microorganisms to Disease," *Quarterly Journal of Microscopical Science*, 1881.

"On Recent Researches with Regard to the Parasitology of Malaria," *British Medical Journal*, 1907.

"On Sulpho-chromic Catgut," *British Medical Journal*, 1909.

About Lister

Guthrie, Douglas. *Lord Lister: His Life and Doctrine*. Baltimore, Md.: Williams & Wilkins, 1949.

Farmer, Laurence. *Master Surgeon: A Biography of Joseph Lister*. New York: Harper, 1962.

Le Fanu, William. *A List of the Original Writings of Joseph, Lord Lister*. Edinburgh, Scotland: Livingstone, 1965.

Fisher, Richard. *Joseph Lister 1827-1912*. New York: Stein & Day, 1977.

(Richard Adler)

Salvador Edward Luria

Disciplines: Bacteriology, biology, cell biology, genetics, and virology

Contribution: Luria's main contribution to molecular biology was in explaining viral replication and gene structure, thus relating virology and biochemistry.

Aug. 13, 1912	Born in Turin, Italy
1929-1935	Attends the University of Turin Medical School
1936-1938	Serves as an officer in the Italian Army Medical Corps
1940	Emigrates to the United States and obtains a position as an assistant at Columbia University Medical School
1943	Instructor at Indiana University's bacteriology department
1943	Publishes "Mutations of Bacteria from Virus Sensitivity to Virus Resistance" with Max Delbrück
1950	Full professor at the University of Illinois at Champaigne-Urbana
1953	Publishes *General Virology* with J. E. Darnell
1959	Becomes chair of the microbiology department at the Massachusetts Institute of Technology (MIT)
1966	Publishes "The Comparative Anatomy of a Gene"
1969	Awarded the Nobel Prize in Physiology or Medicine
1974	Becomes the director of the MIT Center for Cancer Research
Feb. 6, 1991	Dies in Lexington, Massachusetts

Early Life

Salvador Edward Luria was born in 1912 in Turin, Italy, as the second son of Jewish businessman David Luria and Esther Sacerdote Luria. He received his primary and secondary education in the Turin pubic schools. In 1929 Luria was graduated from Liceo d'Azeglio, entered the University of Turin Medical School, and conducted tissue culture research that developed his interest in research science.

In 1935 Luria was graduated *summa cum laude* and became an officer in the Army Medical Corps for three years. He began using mathematics and physics in biological research. On leaving the army, he moved to Paris to avoid Nazi persecution, studied biophysics at the Curie Laboratory, and explored the X-ray mutation of bacteriophages (or phages)—viruses that infect bacteria.

Phages and Fluctuation

In 1940 Luria left France for the United States, arriving in New York City on September 12. He

Bacteriophages

Using fluctuation analysis, Luria showed that resistance to phages occurred prior to the exposure of sensitive bacteria to these bacteria-killing viruses.

Luria studied aspects of the replication and genetic structure of viruses—disease-causing microbes that live and multiply only in the infected cells on which they prey. He worked with viruses called bacteriophages (or phages) that kill bacteria. Whenever a chosen number of "sensitive" bacteria (those that a phage can kill) are grown (cultured) together with phages, the phages soon destroy all the bacteria present.

This occurs because when phages infect bacteria, they turn each infected cell into a virus factory that makes many progeny phages in a short time. The new phages destroy the cell, are released, and infect numerous other bacteria. The cycle of infection and bacterial destruction repeats continually. After several cycles, enough phages are made to destroy all the bacteria in a test culture.

Bacteria unsusceptible to a given phage can be isolated from cultures of sensitive bacteria. An important part of understanding bacterial sensitivity and resistance came from Luria's study of whether resistance to phages arose in a spontaneous fashion or was caused by the action of the phages on unchanged bacteria grown in their presence.

Exploration of this phenomenon was carried out in two steps. First, a large number of bacterial cultures

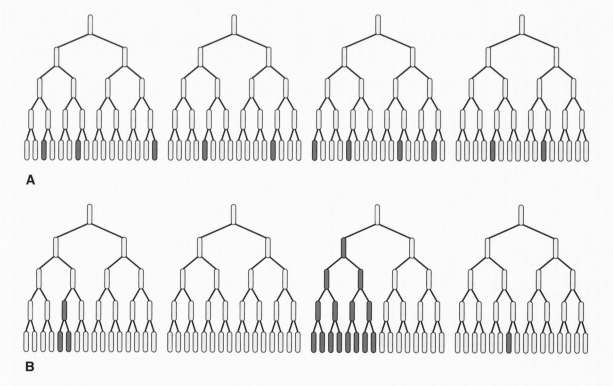

(A). Bacteria become resistant through contact with phages, and their numbers per culture are fairly constant.
(B). They arise spontaneously and their numbers fluctuate greatly between cultures.

of equal size were prepared. Then, the number of resistant bacteria in each one was counted after adding a fixed number of phages and allowing enough time to pass to kill all sensitive bacteria. Luria found that the number of bacterial survivors (resistant cells) varied greatly from culture to culture (see figure).

This fluctuation in the number of survivors indicated that resistant cells arose from events preceding phage exposure. It is now known that its source was spontaneous mutation. Had resistance been the result of the action of the phages on the bacteria, then the number of resistant cells in each culture would have been fairly constant.

The fluctuation test—the observation of variation of the number of resistant cells from culture to culture and its mathematical analysis—has been used to investigate phenomena such as the development of antibiotic resistance in bacteria and the resistance of cancer cells to antitumor drugs. In such cases, resistance has often been shown to develop prior to interaction with these agents. Hence, the procedure has been invaluable to the development of molecular virology, the study of carcinogenesis (the origin of cancer), and an understanding of genetics.

Bibliography

Stent, Gunther. *Molecular Biology of Bacterial Viruses.* San Francisco, Calif.: W. H. Freeman, 1963.

Hayes, William. *The Genetics of Bacteria and Their Viruses.* New York: John Wiley & Sons, 1964.

Luria, Salvador E. *A Slot Machine, a Broken Test Tube.* New York: Harper & Row, 1984.

became an assistant at Columbia University Medical School and continued his bacteriophage research. In 1941 Luria met biophysicist Max Delbrück of the California Institute of Technology (Caltech), and he, Delbrück, and Alfred Day Hershey of Carnegie Institute became a "phage group." They showed that a phage is made of deoxyribonucleic acid (DNA) surrounded by a protein coat and that when phages infect bacteria, the DNA turns them into phage factories.

Luria studied phages as a simple way to test gene alteration. An important discovery arose from this study of bacterial phage resistance. Fluctuation analysis, using Delbrück's mathematical model, was described in the paper "Mutations of Bacteria from Virus Sensitivity to Virus Resistance" (1943). The analysis showed that if virus-sensitive bacteria were grown with phages, the production of resistance fluctuated widely; therefore, it had to occur prior to exposure. Luria's concept of fluctuation analysis reportedly arose on watching a slot machine while he was a bacteriology instructor at the Indiana University. He identified an analogy, if random, between machine payoff and resistant bacteria formation. At Indiana, he married Zella Hurwitz and had a son, Daniel. In 1951, again via Delbrückian mathematics, he showed that during phage growth, mutants arise randomly and spontaneously.

A Nobel Prize and Social Conscience

In 1950, as a full professor at the University of Illinois, Champaign-Urbana, Luria proved that viral genes mutate. Then, in 1959, as microbiology chair at the Massachusetts Institute of Technology (MIT), Luria showed how colicin antibiotics could disrupt cell membrane function by making membrane channels. He, Delbrück, and Hershey shared the 1969 Nobel Prize in Physiology or Medicine for their work on viral replication and gene structure. From 1974, Luria directed MIT's Cancer Research Center.

Socially conscious, he asked Americans to direct technology to the national good. Critical of defense and space program costs, he noted the money for medical research and housing lost to such programs. He gave much of his Nobel Prize award money to opposing the Vietnam War. His honors included the presidency of the American Society of Microbiologists and a National Academy of Science membership. Luria died on February 6, 1991.

Bibliography

By Luria

"Mutations of Bacteria from Virus Sensitivity to Virus Resistance," *Genetics*, 1943 (with Max Delbrück).

"Mutations of Bacterial Viruses Affecting Their Host Range," *Genetics*, 1945.

"Reactivation of Irradiated Bacteriophage by Transfer of Self-Reproducing Units," *Proceedings of the National Academy of Sciences*, 1947.

"Recent Advances in Bacterial Genetics," *Bacteriological Reviews*, 1947.

"Ultraviolet Irradiation During Intracellular Growth," *Journal of Bacteriology*, 1947 (with R. Latarjet).

"Genetic Recombination Leading to Production of Active Bacteriophage from Ultraviolet Inactivated Particles," *Genetics*, 1949 (with Renato Dulbecco).

"The Frequency of Distribution of Spontaneous Bacteriophage Mutants as Evidence for the Exponential Rate of Phage Reproduction," *Cold Spring Harbor Symposia on Quantitative Biology*, 1951.

"Host-Induced Modifications of Bacterial Viruses," *Cold Spring Harbor Symposia on Quantitative Biology*, 1953.

General Virology, 1953 (with J. E. Darnell).

"Lysogenization, Transduction, and Genetic Recombination in Bacteria," *Cold Spring Harbor Symposia on Quantitative Biology*, 1958 (with D. Fraser, J. Adams, and J. Burrows).

"Transduction of Lactose-Utilising Ability Among Strains of *E. coli* and *S. dysenteriae* and the Properties of Transducing Phage Particles," *Virology*, 1960 (with Adams and R. C. Ting).

"The Comparative Anatomy of a Gene," *Harvey Lectures*, 1966.

"Phage, Colicins, and Macroregulatory Phenomena," *Science*, 1970.

Life, the Unfinished Experiment, 1973.

Thirty-six Lectures in Biology, 1975.

A View of Life, 1981 (with Stephen Jay Gould and Sam Singer).

A Slot Machine, a Broken Test Tube: An Autobiography, 1984.

"Genetic Study of the Functional Organization of the Colicin E_1 Molecule," *Journal of Bacteriology*, 1985 (with Joan L. Suit, M. L. Fan, and C. Kaylar).

"Expression of the *kil* Gene of ColE$_1$ Plasmid in *Escherichia coli* kil^r Mutants Causes Release of Periplasmic Enzymes and Colicin Without Cell Death," *Journal of Bacteriology*, 1988 (with Suit).

About Luria

Stent, Gunther. *Molecular Biology of Bacterial Viruses*. San Francisco, Calif.: W H. Freeman, 1963.

Hayes, William. *The Genetics of Bacteria and Their Viruses*. New York: John Wiley & Sons, 1964.

(Sanford S. Singer)

André Lwoff

Disciplines: Biology, genetics, and virology
Contribution: Lwoff's study of lysogenic
viruses played a significant role in the
understanding of the genetic mechanisms
of bacterial replication and viral infection.

May 8, 1902	Born in Ainay-le-Château, France
1921	Receives a bachelor's degree from the Sorbonne
1927	Receives medical degree while working at the Institut Pasteur
1932	Earns a doctorate in the natural sciences
1932	Receives a Rockefeller Fellowship to work at the Kaiser Wilhelm Institute in Heidelberg, Germany
1936	With Marguerite Lwoff, establishes the role of vitamins as coenzymes
1938	Head of the Service de Physiologie Microbienne at the Institut Pasteur
1950	Demonstrates the perpetuation of viral deoxyribonucleic acid (DNA) in lysogenic bacteria
1959	Professor of microbiology at the Sorbonne
1964	Awarded the Médaille de la Résistance for service during World War II
1965	Awarded the Nobel Prize in Physiology or Medicine
1968-1972	Serves as director of the Cancer Research Institute at Vilejuif, near Paris
Sept. 30, 1994	Dies in Paris, France

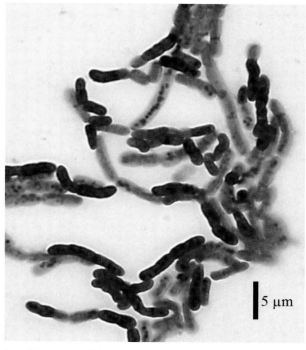

5 μm

Lwoff's study of bacterium helped us understand the spread of disease.

Early Life

André Lwoff (pronounced "lwahf") was born at Ainay-le-Château, France, the son of Russian Jewish immigrants. His father was head physician in a psychiatric hospital and often brought André with him. Lwoff later believed that his inclination toward science resulted from such exposure.

Lwoff developed an interest in biology at the age of thirteen following a visit with Élie Metchnikoff at the Institut Pasteur. Metchnikoff, the founder of the cellular school of immunology, allowed the young student to observe bacteria in his laboratory, and Lwoff decided that his career should be one in medical research.

During the summers of 1920 and 1921, Lwoff spent his time at the Marine Biological Laboratory in Brittany, in addition to studying biology, chemistry, and physics in the Faculté des Sciences in Paris. He received his bachelor's degree in natural sciences from the University of Paris (the Sorbonne) in 1921.

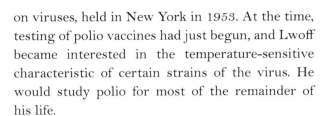

During this time, Lwoff had the opportunity to study with protozoologist Édouard Chatton. It was Chatton who, in 1928, first used the terms "prokaryotic" and "eukaryotic" to describe the two basic forms of cells. Lwoff and Chatton would collaborate until Chatton's death in 1947.

In 1921 Lwoff received a fellowship for the study of protozoa. He continued his research on morphogenesis and development while working for his medical degree. Studying respiration in flagellates, Lwoff was later able to establish the role of hematin as a necessary growth factor, the first example of the role played by vitamins as coenzymes.

During this period, Lwoff developed a friendship with Eugene and Elisabeth Wollman, pioneers in the study of lysogenic bacteria. The Wollmans had established that bacterial viruses (bacteriophages) were introduced into the genetic material of bacteria, a phenomenon called lysogeny. In 1938 Lwoff became chair of microbial physiology at the Institut Pasteur.

The War Years and After

Lwoff remained in France during the war, joining the Resistance. In addition to gathering intelligence for the Allies, he hid American pilots who had been shot down over France. He was later awarded the Médaille de la Résistance for his work. The Wollmans were less fortunate; arrested in 1943, they died in a concentration camp.

In 1949 Lwoff decided to continue the work started by the Wollmans. He demonstrated that single bacteria would carry bacteriophages in an inactive form. The phage, which was incorporated as part of the cell's genetic material, could be induced upon exposure to chemicals or ultraviolet light. This work would result in Lwoff's being awarded the Nobel Prize in Physiology or Medicine in 1965.

Lwoff entered a third phase of his career following his attendance at a Cold Spring Harbor symposium on viruses, held in New York in 1953. At the time, testing of polio vaccines had just begun, and Lwoff became interested in the temperature-sensitive characteristic of certain strains of the virus. He would study polio for most of the remainder of his life.

In 1968 Lwoff retired from the Institut Pasteur, becoming the director of the Cancer Research Institute at Villejuif. He retired in 1972 and died in 1994 at the age of ninety-two.

Bibliography

By Lwoff

"Studies on Codehydrogenases: I. Nature of Growth Factor 'V'," *Proceedings of the Royal Society of London*, 1937 (with M. Lwoff).

L'Évolution physiologique: Étude des pertes de fonctions chez les microorganismes, 1944 (physiological evolution: study of the loss of functions among microorganisms).

Problems of Morphogenesis in Ciliates, 1950.

"Induction de la lyse bactériophagique de la totalité d'une population microbienne lysogène" (induction of lytic bacteriophage from a single population of lysogenic bacteria), *Comptes rendus hebdomadaires des séances de l'Académie des Sciences*, 1950 (with L. Siminovitch and N. Kjeldgaard).

Biochemistry and Physiology of Protozoa, 1951-1964 (3 vols.; as ed).

"Conditions de l'efficacité inductrice du rayonnement ultra-violet chez une bactérie lysogène" (conditions for induction of bacterial lysogen using ultraviolet light), *Annales de l'Institut Pasteur*, 1951.

"Lysogeny," *Bacteriological Reviews*, 1953.

"The Concept of Virus," *Journal of General Microbiology*, 1957.

Biological Order, 1962.

"The Thermosensitive Critical Event of the Viral Cycle," *Cold Spring Harbor Symposia on Quantitative Biology*, 1962.

The Induction of Bacteriophages from Lysogenic Bacteria

Bacterial viruses (bacteriophages) are maintained in a noninfectious form in lysogenic bacteria. Exposure of these bacteria to ultraviolet light can induce the viruses to grow.

Lysogeny, the maintenance of bacteriophages in a noninfectious form, was discovered in 1921 by Jules Bordet and others, who observed that certain strains of bacteria could not be isolated free of the virus. Eugene and Elisabeth Wollman later proposed that these viruses alternate between infectious and noninfectious stages. They also suggested that during the noninfectious stage, the virus is part of the hereditary structure of the bacterium.

In 1949 Lwoff resumed the work started by the Wollmans, both of whom died during World War II. Lwoff believed that the real significance of the lysogenic question was how these lysogenic bacteria maintained the capacity to produce phages in the absence of free virus.

He began his work using a strain of a soil bacterium, *Bacillus megaterium*. He also thought that mass culture of the bacteria could not provide a proper answer. He would have to isolate and cultivate individual cells in order to make his observations.

Lwoff was able to manipulate individual bacteria within a microdrop of growth medium and to transfer these single cells to fresh medium. When the isolated cell had replicated itself into two bacteria, Lwoff would again transfer a single cell to fresh medium. He continued this procedure over the course of nineteen cell divisions.

He found that each isolated cell, even in the absence of free phages, maintained the capacity to produce the virus. Maintenance of lysogeny could not have been the result of phages sticking to the bacterial surface, since an impossibly large number of virus particles would have had to be present in order to survive nineteen divisions.

Lwoff also observed the occasional spontaneous lysis (disintegration) of single bacteria. When he assayed the culture fluid following such lysis, he observed the presence of numerous free bacteriophages. He determined that lysogenic bacteria liberate their phages through lysis. Lwoff's conclusion was that lysogenic bacteria maintain the virus in a noninfectious state, called a prophage.

He also believed that induction of the virus is under the control of environmental factors. He and his students Louis Siminovitch and Niels Kjelgaard began a search of factors that can be used to induce the prophage.

They discovered that irradiation with small doses of ultraviolet light could induce virus production. They also observed similar induction using hydrogen peroxide, X-rays, or certain organic chemicals. Since many of these chemicals have carcinogenic activity, Lwoff at first believed that the induction of such viruses may also play a role in human cancer. Research would later prove this assumption to be incorrect.

Bibliography

Stent, Gunther. *Molecular Biology of Bacterial Viruses.* San Francisco, Calif.: W. H. Freeman, 1963.

Cairns, John, Gunther Stent, and James Watson, eds. *Phage and the Origins of Molecular Biology.* New York: Cold Spring Harbor, 1966.

Darnell, James, Harvey Lodish, and David Baltimore. *Molecular Cell Biology.* New York: W. H. Freeman, 1990.

"Death and Transfiguration of a Problem,"
Bacteriological Reviews, 1969.

"Inhibition of Poliovirus RNA Synthesis by
Supraoptimal Temperatures," *Journal of General
Virology*, 1970.

"From Protozoa to Bacteria and Viruses: Fifty
Years with Microbes," *Annual Review of
Microbiology*, 1971.

*Origins of Molecular Biology: A Tribute to Jacques
Monod*, 1979 (as ed., with Agnes Ullmann).

About Lwoff

Monod, Jacques and Ernest Borek, eds. *Of
Microbes and Life*. New York: Columbia
University Press, 1971.

Magill, Frank N., ed. "André Lwoff," *The Nobel
Prize Winners: Physiology or Medicine*, Pasadena,
Calif.: Salem Press, 1991.

McMurray, Emily J., ed. *Notable Twentieth-Century
Scientists*. Detroit, Mich.: Gale Research, 1995.

(Richard Adler)

Louis Pasteur

Disciplines: Bacteriology, chemistry, immunology, and medicine

Contribution: Pasteur discovered the role of microorganisms in fermentation and invented the food preservation process known as pasteurization. One of the founders of bacteriology, he was the first to inoculate animals and humans against infectious disease successfully.

Dec. 27, 1822	Born in Dole, Jura, France
1843-1847	Studies chemistry and physics at the École Normale Supérieure in Paris
1848	Teaches chemistry at the University of Strasbourg
1854	Professor of chemistry at the University of Lille
1857	Suggests that fermentation is caused by living microorganisms
1857	Assistant director of the École Normale Supérieure
1862	Elected to the Académie des Sciences
1864	Invents pasteurization as a way to prevent wine from spoiling
1867	Proves that diseases of silk-worms are caused by bacteria
1881	Successfully inoculates sheep against anthrax
1882	Elected to the Académie Française
1885	Cures a child of rabies
1888	Founds the Institut Pasteur, serving as its director
Sept. 28, 1895	Dies in Villeneuve-l'Étang, near Saint-Cloud, France

Early Life

Louis Pasteur (pronounced "pahs-TEWR") was born in 1822 in Dole, a small town in eastern France near Dijon, to Jean-Joseph Pasteur, a tanner working from the family home, and Jeanne Roqui Pasteur. Louis attended primary school in Arbois and studied for the *baccalauréat* at Besançon.

Pasteur entered the École Normale Supérieure in Paris in 1843, where he studied chemistry and physics and specialized in crystallography, a field in which he made his first original scientific discovery, molecular asymmetry. After earning a doctorate, he accepted a position as professor of chemistry at the University of Strasbourg in 1848. In 1849 he married Marie Laurent, the daughter of a local academic, who bore five children: Jeanne, Jean-Baptiste, Cécile, Marie-Louise, and Camille.

Early Studies in Microbiology

Pasteur received a membership in the Legion of Honor in 1853 for his research on tartaric acid and rose rapidly through the academic ranks, becoming professor of chemistry and dean of the faculty of the University of Lille in 1854. In 1857 he returned to Paris to accept an appointment as assistant director of the École Normale Supérieure.

Pasteur continued his studies of fermentation and putrefaction in Paris and, at the request of French winemakers, began to examine the causes of alterations in the flavor of wine. He had earlier studied the production of beer for northern French brewers and suspected that microorganisms caused wine to sour, just as they caused beer to spoil. In 1864 he devised a way to prevent spoilage by heating wine, a process now known as pasteurization.

Contagious Diseases in Animals

In 1865 the French government asked Pasteur to study two diseases of silkworms that were harming the French silk industry. He quickly discovered that microorganisms were causing the diseases and suggested the destruction of infected silkworms.

In 1877 he began to search for the microbiological origin of animal and human diseases and decided to study anthrax, a disease of sheep and cattle. Two years later, Pasteur began studying chicken cholera. In the case of both diseases, he discovered methods of immunization.

The chicken cholera studies were especially important. During the experiment, a batch of cholera had spoiled but was still injected into chickens, which then did not become infected. When Pasteur attempted to infect that group of chickens a second time with a properly preserved culture, he discovered the chickens were immune. This experiment led to one of the most important discoveries in the history of medicine. Pasteur loved the saying "chance favors the prepared mind," and he concluded that the chicken cholera microbes had been weakened by being placed in storage. In 1880 Pasteur published an article in which he described the process whereby animals gain immunity to disease when injected with attenuated (weakened) microbes.

Fermentation and Microbiology

Pasteur proved that fermentation is an organic process caused by microscopic living things.

Conventional wisdom in the nineteenth century held that fermentation, like other transformations of organic material such as the souring of milk or the decay of meat, was a chemical process. For example, brewers thought that beer was produced chemically when malts came into contact with the wooden barrels in which it was produced. Although they knew that yeast was present during fermentation, they considered it a by-product with no real role in the process.

In 1853 a local brewer asked Pasteur to discover the cause of spoilage that frequently occurred during fermentation. He accepted the challenge and, by examining fermenting juices under a microscope, discovered that yeasts play the central role in transforming sugar into alcohol. He used the same techniques to study the souring of milk and again concluded that microorganisms are responsible. In 1857 Pasteur published a report in which he argued that microorganisms cause souring and fermentation. In many ways, this paper marks the beginning of modern bacteriology.

In 1859 Pasteur began to study spontaneous generation—the idea, believed by most scientists, that living things could emerge from nonliving matter, such as during the process of fermentation or decay. Pasteur rejected this position and devised many elegant experiments to prove that organic material does not ferment or decay unless it has been exposed to outside influences such as atmospheric air.

His experiments led to a public address at the Sorbonne in 1864 describing experiments showing that neither fermentation nor putrefaction can take place in a solution of organic material that had been sterilized by heat. Pasteur attributed this phenomenon to the absence of living microorganisms in a sterilized medium. Although severely criticized by traditionalists,

Pasteur's laboratory work played a major part in destroying the idea of spontaneous generation and proved that all living things must have parents.

Pasteur found a practical application for his discoveries when French winegrowers asked him to find ways to keep wine from spoiling during fermentation and storage. Pasteur thought that the alteration of fermenting wine (such as its tendency to produce vinegar) and its spoilage during storage resulted from the presence of microorganisms in the wine. He verified this theory through microscopic examination and determined that wine could be preserved from alteration if unwanted microorganisms could be eliminated.

Pasteur first tried to kill the microorganisms by adding chemical disinfectants. These experiments failed, but he soon discovered that heating wine to 55 degrees Celsius kills the microorganisms without damaging the flavor of the wine. Pasteur's process of partial sterilization, now commonly known as pasteurization, is widely used to prevent spoilage in milk and other foods.

Bibliography

Conant, James Bryant. "Pasteur's Study of Fermentation," *Harvard Case Histories in Experimental Science.* Vol. 2. Cambridge, Mass.: Harvard University Press, 1957.

Farley, John and Gerald L. Geison. "Science, Politics, and Spontaneous Generation in Nineteenth-Century France: The Pasteur-Pouchet Debate," *Bulletin of the History of Medicine* 48 (1974).

Dubos, René. *Pasteur and Modern Science.* Madison, Wis.: Science Tech Publishers, 1988.

Latour, Bruno. *The Pasteurization of France.* Cambridge, Mass.: Harvard University Press, 1988.

Immunization

Pasteur had many professional enemies who reject-ed his theories about the role of microorganisms in disease, despite his writings and arguments. He decided to win them over by a public demonstra-tion. In 1881 he invited his detractors to witness an inoculation at a farm near Pouilly-le-Fort, close to the town of Melun, southeast of Paris. There, Pasteur showed that sheep inoculated with attenuated anthrax microbes could survive later inoculation with active microbes.

Pasteur's success in inoculating animals prompted him to begin experiments on rabies, a disease that brought certain death to infected humans. Pasteur cultured the rabies virus in the spinal cords of rabbits, and discovered ways to bring it to a high state of virulence and then attenuate it by drying the spinal cords in the presence of oxygen. In 1884 he successfully inoculated dogs against the disease.

The next year, Pasteur achieved his greatest triumph as a microbiologist. The parents of a young boy who had been bitten by a rabid dog came to Pasteur and asked for help. Although Pasteur had never inoculated a human before, he knew that the boy certainly would die without treatment. He inoculated him with successively stronger doses of attenuated microbes. Pasteur's experiment succeeded: the boy, Joseph Meister, survived.

Recognition

Unlike many scientists, Pasteur received ample recognition during his lifetime. His colleagues elected him to the Académie des Sciences in 1862 and to the Académie du Médecine in 1873. In 1882 he won election to the Académie Française, France's most prestigious scholarly organization. His career culminated in 1888 with the opening of the Institut Pasteur, a research institute devoted to combating infectious diseases.

When Pasteur died of kidney disease in 1895, he was universally recognized as one of the preeminent scientists of his age.

Bibliography

By Pasteur

"Mémoire sur les corpuscules organisés qui existent dans l'atmosphère, examen de la doctrine des générations spontanées," *Annales des sciences naturelles*, 1861.

Études sur le vin: ses maladies, causes qui les provoquent, 1866.

Études sur la maladie des vers à soie: moyen pratique assuré de la combattre et d'en prévenir le retour, 1870 (2 vols.).

Études sur la bière: ses maladies, causes qui les provoquent, procédé pour la rendre inaltérable, avec une théorie nouvelle de la fermentation, 1876 (*Studies on Fermentation: The Diseases of Beer, Their Causes, and the Means of Preventing Them*, 1879).

"Charbon et septicémie," *Comptes rendus*, 1877 (with J. F Joubert).

Oeuvres de Pasteur, 1922-1939 (Pasteur Vallery-Radot, ed.).

Correspondance, 1940-1951 (4 vols.; Vallery-Radot, ed.; *Correspondence of Pasteur and Thuillier Concerning Anthrax and Swine Fever Vaccinations*, 1968).

About Pasteur

Duclaux, Émile. *Pasteur: The History of a Mind.* Trans. by Erwin F. Smith and Florence Hedges. Philadelphia, Pa.: W. B. Saunders, 1920.

Vallery-Radot, René. *The Life of Pasteur.* Trans. by Mrs. R. L. Devonshire. 2 vols. New York: Doubleday, 1923.

Dubos, René. *Louis Pasteur: Free Lance of Science.* Boston. Mass.: Little, Brown, 1950.

Vallery-Radot, Pasteur. *Pasteur: A Great Life in Brief.* Trans. by Alfred Joseph. New York: Alfred A. Knopf, 1966.

Geison, Gerald L. *The Private Science of Louis Pasteur.* Princeton, N.J.: Princeton University Press, 1995.

(C. James Haug)

The Germ Theory of Disease

Pasteur, along with Robert Koch of Germany, proved the central role of germs in causing many diseases. Pasteur's main contribution lay in demonstrating the efficacy of immunization.

Before the last half of the nineteenth century, it was widely believed that disease could not be transmitted directly from one person or animal to another. Instead, most physicians thought that epidemic diseases were caused by nonliving agents called "miasma" produced by the decomposition of organic materials. In essence, the miasmatic theory of disease stated that bad smells caused epidemic diseases such as typhoid fever and cholera. Physicians counseled their patients to avoid coming near such things as decaying vegetation, manure, and carcasses. If this was not possible, they suggested overwhelming the foul odors with camphor and sweet-smelling spices.

By the 1870s, Pasteur's research into fermentation and putrefaction had led him to conclude that all transformations of organic materials are caused by microorganisms. From this point of view, disease is simply another transformation of organic material.

His studies of the microbial causes of human and animal diseases were preceded by a study of disease in insects. In 1865 the French government had asked Pasteur to study two diseases of silkworms, called *pébrine* and *flâcherie*, that were devastating the French silk industry. He began research at Alais, in southern France, and quickly discovered that microorganisms caused the diseases.

In 1877 Pasteur began to study anthrax, a disease that mainly affects sheep and cattle. Although Koch had explained the etiology of anthrax in an 1876 study, many scientists thought that the disease killed animals by producing a chemical poison. Pasteur discovered that animals contract anthrax by grazing in fields where contaminated blood from dead infected animals has soaked into the soil. The spores of anthrax, Pasteur showed, are brought to the surface of the soil by earthworms.

Pasteur's main contribution to the germ theory of disease lay not in the discovery of disease-causing organisms but in devising ways to confer immunity. In 1879 he began to study chicken cholera, a disease unrelated to human cholera. Pasteur identified the causative microbe and began experimenting with cultures of different virulence. He accidently injected laboratory chickens with a sample of culture that had been stored for several weeks. These chickens injected suffered few ill effects and later survived an otherwise lethal dose of virulent culture. A serendipitous discovery: the weakened microbes could cause illness, but not death, and animals injected with them gained immunity from the disease. This discovery marked a pivotal point in the research of immunology.

In 1881 Pasteur conducted a dramatic public experiment to demonstrate the efficacy of his anthrax vaccine. He inoculated twenty-five sheep with attenuated anthrax microbes. Two weeks later, he injected these sheep and twenty-five others with fresh, active microbes. All twenty-five inoculated animals survived; all those not inoculated perished. Pasteur's critics left the field convinced. The ability of germs to cause disease and the effectiveness of immunization could no longer be questioned.

Bibliography

Foster, W. D. *A History of Medical Bacteriology and Immunology.* London: William Heinemann, 1970.

Bulloch, W. *The History of Bacteriology.* New York: Dover, 1977.

Pasteur, Louis. *Germ Theory and Its Applications to Medicine and Surgery.* H. C. Ernst, trans. Buffalo, N.Y.: Prometheus Books, 1996.

Stanley B. Prusiner

Discipline: Neurology

Contribution: Best known for the discovery of prions—infectious pathogens which cause neurodegenerative diseases in animals and humans.

May 28, 1942	Born in Des Moines, Iowa
1966	Graduates *cum laude* from University of Pennsylvania
1968	Earns M.D. from University of Pennsylvania School of Medicine
1968	Internship in Medicine at University of California, San Francisco (UCSF)
1969	Wins appointment at the National Institutes of Health (NIH)
1972	Begins residency at UCSF, in Neurology
1974	Accepts position in Neurology at UCSF
1982	Publishes article about his identification of prions
1991	Receives the Potamkin Prize for Alzheimer's Disease Research
1992	Receives Bristol-Myers Squibb Award for Distinguished Achievement in Neuroscience
1997	Awarded the Nobel Prize in Physiology or Medicine for the identification of prions
2010	Awarded the National Medal of Science

Prusiner discovered the infectious pathogens prions.

Early Life

Stanley Prusiner was born in Des Moines, Iowa, to Lawrence and Miriam Prusiner in 1942. Shortly after, his father was drafted into the United States Navy, and for a short time the family lived in Boston, Massachusetts, while Lawrence attended naval officer training school.

During World War II, while his father was on duty, Prusiner and his mother moved to Cincinnati, Ohio, where his maternal grandmother lived. The family was reunited when the war ended and decided to stay in Cincinnati, where Lawrence practiced architecture for the next twenty-five years, enabling a comfortable upbringing for the Prusiner family.

Prusiner was not a particularly motivated high-school student, though he did take an interest in Latin while attending Walnut Hills High School. However, his grades earned him acceptance into the University of Pennsylvania, where he majored in chemistry.

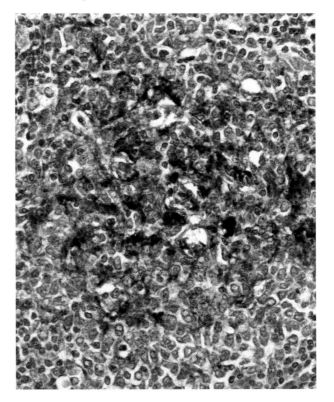

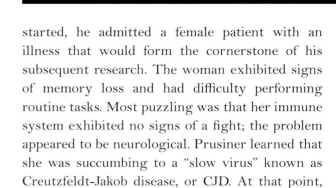

What the high school experience lacked, the college more than made up for. Prusiner thrived on the intellectual stimulation that the University of Pennsylvania offered. He took classes with renowned professors in philosophy and economics, and delved deeper into his heritage through the history of architecture and Russian history. He was also heavily involved with the university's crew team.

A Passion for Research

In the summer of 1963 Prusiner began to solidify his path as a future researcher. Along with Sidney Wolfson in the Department of Surgery, he started a research project on hypothermia, which he worked on through his senior year. The experience of working with Wolfson on the project proved to be so engaging that Prusiner decided to stay at Pennsylvania and attend medical school.

As a medical student, he undertook research on the fluorescence of brown fat and the metabolism of isolated brown adipocytes at the Wenner-Gren Institute in Stockholm, Sweden, with Olav Lindberg. The excitement of his research experience caused him to give serious thought to a career in biomedical research.

In 1968 Prusiner completed medical school and accepted an internship at the University of California, San Francisco (UCSF). He also gained the opportunity to work at the National Institutes of Health (NIH) for three years, studying *E. coli*. Being at the NIH played a pivotal role in his understanding of the research process, where he learned to write clear manuscripts and document discovery using multiple approaches. It was near the end of his time at NIH that he decided to pursue neurology.

Studying the Slow Virus

In 1972 Prusiner began his residency at the University of California, San Francisco, in the Department of Neurology. Shortly after he started, he admitted a female patient with an illness that would form the cornerstone of his subsequent research. The woman exhibited signs of memory loss and had difficulty performing routine tasks. Most puzzling was that her immune system exhibited no signs of a fight; the problem appeared to be neurological. Prusiner learned that she was succumbing to a "slow virus" known as Creutzfeldt-Jakob disease, or CJD. At that point, scientists were not certain that a virus was the actual cause because of the unusual properties of the responsible infectious agent.

Prusiner became captivated with the idea of identifying the molecular structure of this mysterious agent. He became passionate about researching CJD and other slow-virus illnesses, reading as much as he could on the subject. Prior research had revealed that similar brain diseases such as kuru, a rare degenerative disease seen in the Fore people of New Guinea, and scrapie, a slow virus affecting sheep, could be contracted through the introduction of infected brain matter. Working with the scrapie agent, he started to map out a research agenda and brainstormed methods for further investigation.

By this time, Prusiner had met his wife, Sandy, and accepted a position at UCSF in the Department of Neurology in 1974. There he worked on setting up a laboratory to further study scrapie. He managed to obtain some modest funding for his studies by collaborating with two colleagues at the Rocky Mountain Laboratory in Montana, William Hadlow and Carl Eklund, who taught him a great deal about scrapie and the scrapie agent.

A Struggle for Understanding

Unfortunately, Prusiner faced many difficulties while attempting to learn more about scrapie. His research was beginning to feel pointless: data from the research produced puzzling results, showing what he thought was a small virus lacking nucleic acid. Funding from the Howard Hughes Medical

Creutzfeldt-Jakob Disease (CJD)

The illness, which affects about one person in every one million per year globally, was first characterized in 1920 by German neurologist Hans Gerhard Creutzfeldt and shortly afterwards by Alfons Maria Jakob.

Creutzfeldt-Jakob disease (CJD) is a fatal and degenerative brain disorder characterized by rapidly progressive dementia. Though the symptoms appear similar to other neurological illnesses, such as Huntington's and Alzheimer's disease, people with CJD tend to exhibit more aggressive mental impairment. The disease has a long incubation period, often up to 50 years. There are about 200 cases per year in the United States.

CJD appears in one of three categories: sporadic, hereditary, and acquired. Sporadic CJD is the most common, accounting for about 85 percent of cases, and develops despite the absence of any risk factors for the disease. In hereditary CJD, which accounts for 5-10 percent of U.S. cases, there is a family history and/or test results are positive for a genetic mutation associated with CJD. Aquired CJD is characterized by exposure to brain or nervous system tissue, general through medical procedures. Since its discovery, less than 1 percent of cases are of this type.

Variant CJD (vCJD) appears to be related to bovine spongiform encephalopathy (BSE), also known as "mad cow" disease, in lab tests. This differs from classic CJD in that the age of those affected tends to be younger than average. Several cases were documented in Great Britain and France, leading to a theorized link between BSE and the consumption of contaminated beef.

Bibliography

"Cruetzfeldt-Jakob Disease Fact Sheet," National Institute of Neurological Disorders and Stroke, http://www.ninds.nih.gov/disorders/cjd/detail_cjd.htm

Institute (HHMI) was pulled, and UCSF did not grant him tenure. The situation began to brighten, though, when the tenure decision was reversed and he gained a new source of private funding from the R. J. Reynolds Company.

With the increased funding and a large accumulation of data, Prusiner became more confident in his findings, and wrote an article summarizing his work that was published in the April 1982 edition of *Science*. In the article, he introduced the new term "prion," a derivation of proteinaceous infectious particle. Prions differed from pathogens such as viruses and fungi because they contained no DNA or RNA. These proteins are normally found in cells but in some cases can transform into disease-causing forms, such as with CJD in humans and bovine spongiform encephalopthy, or "mad cow" disease, in cattle. The discovery also served as a useful tool in studying other proteins, such as those found in the brains of Alzheimer's patients.

News of the discovery conjured a slew of detractors, with virologists cringing in disbelief, and scrapie and CJD investigators thoroughly angered. Prusiner became the target of vicious attacks in the media. He and colleague Detlev Reisner, wanting to be exhaustive in their research, looked tirelessly for any evidence of nucleic acid.

Prusiner continued his work, collaborating with Charles Weissman on the molecular cloning of the prion protein (PrP). He and his team produced antibodies, enabling them to study the disease in transgenic mice. The early 1990s brought with it a wider acceptance of the existence of prions by many in the scientific community, and Prusiner began to be recognized for his work, gathering accolades such as the Potamkin Prize for Alzheimer's Disease Research in 1991 and the Nobel Prize for Physiology or Medicine in 1997. Prusiner also has fifty issued or allowed patents, and all are assigned to the University of California.

In recent years, Prusiner has focused his energy on the lack of funding for and attention given to Alzheimer's research, alleging that while there are 500,000 new cases of Alzheimer's each year, funding for cancer research is about 15 times greater.

Bibliography

By Prusiner

"Novel proteinaceous infectious particles cause scrapie," *Science* 9. Vol. 216, no. 4542, pp.136-144 (1982).

"Prions," *Proceedings of the National Academy of Sciences*. Vol. 95, pp. 13363-13383 (1998).

About Prusiner

"Stanley B. Prusiner—Biographical," Nobelprize. org, http://www.nobelprize.org/nobel_prizes/ medicine/laureates/1997/prusiner-bio.html

"Long-Time NIH Grantee Stanley B. Prusiner Wins Nobel Prize," http://www.ninds.nih.gov/ news_and_events/news_articles/pressrelease_ prions_100697.htm

"The Scourge of Alzheimer's and Parkinson's and Prion Diseases," Santa Clara University College of Arts and Sciences, http://www.scu.edu/cas/ enrichment/denardo/prusiner.cfm

Ruggles, Rick, "Nobel laureate Stanley Prusiner says U.S. neglects Alzheimer's research," *Omaha World-Herald*, December 14, 2012, http:// www.omaha.com/article/20121213/ LIVEWELL01/712149944

Walter Reed

Disciplines: Bacteriology and medicine

Contribution: Reed was an U.S. Army bacteriologist and pathologist who directed the experiments which established that yellow fever is transmitted by the bite of an *Aedes aegypti* mosquito.

Sept. 13, 1851	Born in Belroi, Virginia
1869	Receives an M.D. from the University of Virginia
1870	Receives a second M.D. from Bellevue Medical College
1876-1888	Serves various posts as an army garrison physician in the West
1889	Appointed attending surgeon and examiner of recruits for Baltimore, Maryland
1890-1891	Studies pathology at Johns Hopkins University
1893	Curator of the Army Medical Museum
1894	Professor of bacteriology at the Army Medical School
1898	Chairs a committee to investigate typhoid fever in military camps
1899	Begins to investigate yellow fever
1900	With James Carroll, submits his final report on a bacillus isolated by Giuseppe Sanarelli
1900	Establishes a research station on yellow fever in Cuba
Nov. 22, 1902	Dies in Washington, D.C.

Early Life

Walter Reed was born in Belroi, Virginia, in 1851. He enrolled at the University of Virginia, intending to study classics. After a brief period, however, he transferred to the medical faculty and completed his course of study in nine months. In 1869, at the age of eighteen, he received the doctor of medicine degree. He then enrolled at Bellevue Medical College in New York and earned a second medical degree.

After serving as an intern and district physician, Reed entered the U.S. Army in 1875. He served in remote outposts for many years. Reed was named the curator of the Army Medical Museum in 1893 and a professor of bacteriology in the newly established Army Medical School the following year. During the Spanish-American War of 1898, he investigated typhoid fever in military camps. The following year, he became involved in the problem of yellow fever.

Reed's work demonstrated that yellow fever was transmitted by the bite of a *Aedes aegypti* mosquito.

The Yellow Fever Years

Yellow fever is known to be transmitted by the bite of a mosquito that carries the virus that causes the disease. Proving this chain of events occupied the latter years of Reed's life. Prior to Reed's work, the disease was thought to be transmitted by simple contact with objects such as bedding and clothing that were contaminated with yellow fever.

The U.S. Army assigned Reed and James Carroll to investigate an organism, *Bacillus icteroides*, which the Italian bacteriologist Giuseppe Sanarelli claimed to have isolated from yellow fever patients. In April, 1899, Reed and Carroll submitted their first report on the yellow fever organism. In February, 1900, they published their final report, showing that Sanarelli's bacillus actually causes a variety of cholera in swine. It was only an accidental or secondary invader among individuals with yellow fever. The causative organism for yellow fever had not yet been identified.

Reed was assigned to investigate an outbreak of malaria in Havana, Cuba. After an initial review of the situation and examinations of those who were sick, he correctly diagnosed the disease as yellow fever. At this point, Reed decided to explore the possibility of insects spreading yellow fever as intermediate hosts. He made these suggestions in a report. The U.S. Army provided resources to conduct experiments concerning the transmission of yellow fever, and also noted that William Gorgas was struggling with this disease among the workers constructing a canal in Panama.

Reed established a research facility 300 miles from Havana. He recruited volunteers and systematically conducted his experiments. Under controlled situations, Reed exposed his volunteers to a variety of mosquitoes, people infected with yellow fever, and personal items that had been used by individuals who had died from the disease.

Over the next few months, Reed demonstrated that the *Aedes aegypti* mosquito transmitted the causative agent for yellow fever. Applying this

The Transmission of Yellow Fever

Reed applied epidemiological principles to identify a certain type of mosquito as the vector for yellow fever and then to modify the environment to eliminate breeding sites for these mosquitoes.

Yellow fever is an acute viral disease characterized by a sudden onset of nausea, moderate fever, slowed heart rate, vomiting of blood, jaundice, and reduced urine output. Blood oozes from the gums, and the tongue turns strawberry red. These symptoms are followed by a severe headache and a high fever (104 degrees Fahrenheit or more). The disease has a fatality rate of up to 20 percent in untreated populations. Yellow fever has an incubation period of three to six days; the clinical disease typically lasts for two to three days. Full recovery in another two days is the rule.

In 1900, while conducting research in Cuba, Reed systematically studied a group of human volunteers over a period of a few months. He found that individuals bitten by *Aedes aegypti* mosquitoes that had previously fed on volunteers who had yellow fever became ill. Reed imported *Aedes aegypti* mosquitoes from areas that were free of yellow fever. Volunteers who were bitten by these mosquitoes did not develop the disease.

This demonstration showed that the *Aedes aegypti* mosquito was a vector responsible for spreading yellow fever. Further, Reed showed that the cause was not inherent in the mosquito but was something, most likely a microorganism, carried by it. Yellow fever could be eradicated if the mosquitoes could be exterminated. Engineering projects in Cuba to destroy the breeding grounds for mosquitoes, consisting mainly of draining swampy areas and eliminating standing water, were begun in 1901. Within three months, Havana was free of the disease.

Yellow fever is found in South America and in tropical areas of west, central, and east Africa. There are two distinct variants of yellow fever: the urban and sylvan (jungle) forms. The urban form is transmitted from person to person by the *Aedes aegypti* mosquito.

A Comparison of Mosquitoes that Transmit Disease

Mosquito	Habits	Features	Diseases
Aedes	Day biter, urban or rural	Head bent, body parallel to surface, black and white in color	Dengue, yellow fever, viral encephalitis
Anopheles	Night biter, mainly rural	Head and body in line, at angle to surface	Malaria, filariasis

The sylvan form is maintained by passage between monkeys and forest canopy mosquitoes; yellow fever is transmitted to humans when they enter the jungle. Clinically, the two varieties do not differ.

As of 1997, urban yellow fever had not occurred in the Western Hemisphere since 1954. It remained common, however, in Africa, particularly in urban centers; an average of two to three major epidemics occurred in Africa each decade since 1960. The *Aedes aegypti* mosquito breeds in small amounts of standing water such as that found in cans, tires, and puddles. Tires can transport dried eggs that hatch when water becomes available. Because of resistance to pesticides, and the high price of labor, control is often difficult, and urban yellow fever has returned to the Western Hemisphere. Rio de Janeiro, once free of the mosquito, became reinfested.

An effective vaccine is available for yellow fever. It has been used in Asia to eliminate the disease despite the presence of *Aedes aegypti* mosquitoes. Treatment of the disease involves bed rest and the replacement of fluid and blood losses. Local measures to control yellow fever exposure include mosquito netting and repellants.

Bibliography

Strode, G. K., ed. *Yellow Fever.* New York: McGraw Hill, 1951.

Monath, T. P. *"Yellow Fever: A Medically Neglected Disease."* Review of Infectious Diseases 9 (1987).

Benenson, A. S. *Control of Communicable Diseases in Man.* 16th ed. Washington, D.C.: American Public Health Association, 1995.

knowledge, he decided to interrupt the disease cycle by eliminating the intermediate host. Within three months, Havana was free of yellow fever.

The same technology was then applied in Panama, where yellow fever was greatly slowing progress on construction of the Panama Canal. After the swamps were drained, both the mosquito population and yellow fever were eliminated.

Reed returned to Washington, D.C., from Havana and resumed his teaching duties. He died on November 22, 1902, following an operation for appendicitis.

Bibliography

By Reed

The Etiology of Yellow Fever: An Additional Note, 1902 (with James Carroll and Aristides Agramonte).

Report on the Origin and Spread of Typhoid Fever in U.S. Military Camps During the Spanish War of 1898, 1904 (with Victor C. Vaughan and Edward O. Shakespeare).

About Reed

Wood, Leonard N. *Doctors in Uniform.* New York: Julian Messner, 1943.

Edelson, Edwin. *Healers in Uniform.* New York: Doubleday, 1971.

(L. Fleming Fallon, Jr.)

Peyton Rous

Disciplines: Biology, genetics, and virology

Contribution: Rous was the first to demonstrate that cancer in animals can be caused by viruses. His discovery resulted in his being awarded the 1966 Nobel Prize in Physiology or Medicine.

Oct. 5, 1879	Born in Baltimore, Maryland
1900	Earns a B.A. at Johns Hopkins University
1904–1906	Serves as resident house officer at The Johns Hopkins Hospital
1905	Awarded a medical degree from Johns Hopkins University
1906–1908	Becomes an instructor in pathology at the University of Michigan
1909	Accepts a position as an assistant member at the Rockefeller Institute for Medical Research
1910	Demonstrates that sarcomas in chickens are caused by a "filterable agent"
1920–1945	Member in pathology and bacteriology at the Rockefeller Institute
1920–1970	Editor of the *Journal of Experimental Medicine*
1927	Elected to the National Academy of Sciences
1945	Member emeritus of the Rockefeller Institute
1957–1970	Serves on the board of consultants at the Sloan-Kettering Institute
1966	Awarded the Nobel Prize in Physiology or Medicine
Feb. 16, 1970	Dies in New York

Early Life

Francis Peyton Rous (pronounced "rows") was born in Baltimore to Charles and Frances Rous. His father died when Peyton was eleven, and his mother decided to remain in Baltimore to take advantage of the educational opportunities. It was there that Rous grew to adulthood.

Rous demonstrated an early interest in science. In his teens, he wrote a "flower of the month" column for the *Baltimore Sun*. Interest in biology led him to enroll at Johns Hopkins University, from which he was graduated in 1900. Rous then entered the medical school there, earning his M.D. in 1905.

During his residency at the hospital, Rous decided that his interests lay in research rather than in treatment of illness. In 1906 he began a period of study on blood cells with Aldred Warthin at the University of Michigan, followed by a summer of study in Germany. Returning to the United States in 1909, Rous contracted tuberculosis and was forced to recuperate in an Adirondacks sanatorium.

The Rockefeller Institute

In 1909 Simon Flexner, the director of the newly established Rockefeller Institute for Medical Research, asked Rous to come to New York and carry out cancer research. Rous would remain associated with the institute (later Rockefeller University) until his death.

Shortly after Rous joined the institute, a chicken with a large breast tumor was brought to him. Rous prepared cell-free filtrates from the tumor and demonstrated that these filtrates would cause similar tumors when injected into healthy chickens. This work, published in the *Journal of Experimental Medicine* in 1910, was the first to demonstrate that cancer in animals is transmissible.

Difficulties in repeating his work when studying other forms of mammalian tumors, however, resulted in Rous abandoning this line of research in 1915. During World War I, he was instrumental in developing a means to preserve and transfuse blood. He traveled to France and created the first blood bank, using blood donated by soldiers.

The study of blood represented a new area of research for Rous. Following the war, his interests entered the area of physiology, reflected in the variety of projects with which he became associated: capillary permeability in muscles, gallstone formation, and the function of the gallbladder.

In 1933 Richard Shope of the Rockefeller Institute discovered a virus that caused warts (papillomas) in rabbits. Rous soon established that the papilloma was actually a tumor. He would continue to study this topic for most of the remainder of his career.

Awards and Recognition

Understanding of the significance of Rous's 1910 discovery of what would be known as the Rous sarcoma virus was a long time in coming. Eventually, the role of viruses in some forms of cancer would be recognized; Rous received the

The Isolation of Tumor Virus from Animals

Rous' isolation of a tumor virus from chickens in 1910 represented the first demonstration that cancer can be caused by a virus.

At the beginning of the twentieth century, the concept of viruses was still unclear. They had never actually been seen, and the possibility that they could cause cancer was not even considered.

A local farmer brought a Plymouth Rock chicken with a large breast tumor to the Rockefeller Institute. Rous determined that the tumor was a sarcoma, a type of cancer associated with connective tissue. He prepared an extract from the tumor and passed the material through a filter to remove any cells or bacteria. When he injected the cell-free filtrate into other chickens, they too developed sarcomas.

Rous's conclusions were not initially accepted by much of the scientific community. The feeling was that the work had been sloppy, that either bacteria or tumor cells had also passed through the filter. Rous also proved unable to repeat the work using mammalian tumors, and he eventually moved into other areas of research.

The isolation of other tumor viruses some decades later would vindicate Rous. His initial isolate became known as the Rous sarcoma virus and would play a key role in the study of genes associated with cancer.

Bibliography

Bishop, J. Michael. "The Molecular Genetics of Cancer," *Science* 235 (1987).

Varmus, Harold. *Genes and the Biology of Cancer.* New York: W. H. Freeman, 1993.

Weinberg, Robert. *Racing to the Beginning of the Road.* New York: Harmony Books, 1996.

Nobel Prize in Physiology or Medicine in 1966 as a result of his contributions.

Rous was awarded nine honorary degrees over the course of his career. Among the other major honors bestowed on him were the John Scott Medal in 1927, the Walker Prize from the Royal College of Surgeons in 1942, the Kovalenko Medal in 1956, the Lasker Award in 1958, and the National Medal of Science in 1966. He died in 1970.

Bibliography

By Rous

"A Transmissible Avian Neoplasm (Sarcoma of the Common Fowl)," *Journal of Experimental Medicine*, 1910.

"A Sarcoma of the Fowl Transmissible by an Agent Separable from the Tumor Cells," *Journal of Experimental Medicine*, 1911.

"The Preservation of Living Red Blood Cells in vitro: I. Methods of Preservation," *Journal of Experimental Medicine*, 1916 (with J. Turner).

"The Preservation of Living Red Blood Cells in vitro: II. The Transfusion of Kept Cells," *Journal of Experimental Medicine*, 1916 (with Turner).

The Modern Dance of Death, 1929.

"A Virus-Induced Mammalian Growth with the Characters of a Tumor," *Journal of Experimental Medicine*, 1934 (with J. Beard).

About Rous

A Notable Career in Finding Out: Peyton Rous 1879-1970. New York: Rockefeller University Press, 1971.

Magill, Frank N., ed. "Peyton Rous," *The Nobel Prize Winners: Physiology or Medicine*. Pasadena, Calif.: Salem Press, 1991.

McMurray, Emily J., ed. *Notable Twentieth-Century Scientists*. Detroit, Mich.: Gale Research, 1995.

(Richard Adler)

Jonas Salk

Disciplines: Immunology, medicine, and virology

Contribution: Salk developed the first effective vaccine used for the prevention of polio. His earlier research also contributed to an understanding of influenza infection.

Oct. 28, 1914	Born in New York
1934	Graduated from the City College of New York
1939	Receives a medical degree from the New York University School of Medicine
1942	Given a National Research Fellowship at the University of Michigan
1947-1964	Appointed head of the Virus Research Laboratory at the University of Pittsburgh
1952	Tests his first prototype vaccine against poliomyelitis at the Watson Home for Crippled Children, reporting his results in *Journal of the American Medical Association*
1954	Nationwide field trials of the Salk vaccine are conducted
Apr. 12, 1955	The success of vaccine field trials is announced
1963	Appointed director of the Salk Institute for Biological Studies in La Jolla, California
1972-1973	Publishes *Man Unfolding* and *The Survival of the Wisest*
June 23, 1995	Dies in La Jolla, California

Early Life

Jonas Edward Salk was born in New York City in 1914, the eldest of three sons of Daniel and Doris Salk. Soon after his birth, the family moved to an apartment in the Bronx, where Salk attended school.

Salk showed early promise in the sciences, attending Townsend Harris High School, which specialized in teaching students with exceptional potential. At the time, Salk was more interested in a law career but, after enrolling in City College at the age of fifteen, he observed the beauty and intricacies of science and decided to make medicine his career.

After his graduation from City College in 1934, he enrolled in the New York University (NYU) School of Medicine. Salk received his medical degree in 1939.

Research in Virology

During Salk's first year in medical school, he was awarded a fellowship for studies in protein chemistry, learning techniques that he would use in his vaccine studies in later years. He also had the opportunity to meet Thomas Francis, Jr., a prominent bacteriologist who had recently arrived from the Rockefeller Institute. Francis was interested in the production of vaccines, particularly one against influenza (flu). In this manner, Salk was introduced both to the concept of immunology and to the complexities of virus replication.

One summer, working in a laboratory at Woods Hole, Massachusetts, while in medical school, Salk met Donna Lindsay, a student in the School of Social Work at NYU. They married in 1939, the day after Salk's graduation. Although the marriage ended in divorce in 1968, they had three sons. In 1970 Salk married painter Françoise Gilot, a former companion of artist Pablo Picasso and the mother of two of Picasso's children.

Salk had hoped to remain in New York and sought a residency at various hospitals, but the anti-Semitic attitude that was pervasive at the time prevented any such appointment. Instead, when Salk was awarded a National Research Council Fellowship in 1942, he joined Francis in Michigan. During this period, he perfected his techniques of vaccine production, developing with Francis several commercial flu vaccines. The work was considered as an important contribution to the war effort during World War II.

The Fight Against Poliomyelitis

In 1947 Salk joined the staff at the University of Pittsburgh as director of virus research. He also changed the emphasis of his work from influenza to the study of poliomyelitis (polio).

An ancient disease, paralytic polio was a devastating illness. Striking seemingly without warning, polio could leave a child paralyzed for life, and was sometimes fatal. In the early decades of the twentieth century, polio epidemics came with increasing regularity; in 1952, 58,000 cases and 3,000 deaths were reported in the United States alone.

A Polio Vaccine

Salk turned his attention to vaccine production in 1949. First, he inactivated the virus by treating it with formalin. Once the logistics were worked out, Salk was ready to test a preliminary vaccine on children. After determining its safety by first injecting himself and his family, Salk tested the prototype vaccine at the Watson Home for Crippled Children in 1952. It proved successful.

In 1954 Salk began nationwide field studies of his vaccine. The trials were coordinated through the University of Michigan. Some 1.8 million children would participate.

On April 12, 1955, Salk announced the results of the field trials at a press conference held in Ann Arbor, Michigan. The vaccine worked. Its efficacy became clear in subsequent years, as the number of new polio cases dropped sharply each year.

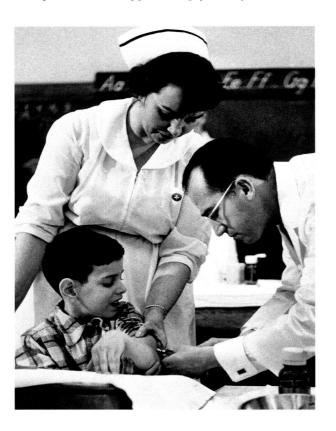

A Polio Vaccine

Salk developed the first effective vaccine that would immunize persons against poliomyelitis.

Although several attempts had been made before Salk to develop a vaccine to combat poliomyelitis (polio), none were both safe and effective. As the twentieth century progressed, the disease struck with increasing frequency: as many as 50,000 people, mostly children, were being diagnosed with the illness each year.

It was against this background that Salk began his work. The initial problem was that of organization. Research into the disease and its cause was disjointed. It was only in the early 1940s that the fecal-oral method of transmission became understood. By the late 1940s, it was still unclear exactly how many strains of the virus even existed; some estimates placed the number in the hundreds.

Such background research was important. As early as 1931, Frank Macfarlane Burnet had shown that monkeys that were immune to one type of the virus could still be infected by other strains. Funded through the National Foundation for Infantile Paralysis, often referred to as the March of Dimes, Salk and other scientists became part of a team to determine how many varieties of the virus existed.

Salk and his co-workers began his typing study in 1949. By the end of the year, much of the confusion had been cleared up; Salk had found that despite dozens of minor varieties, there were probably only three strains of the virus.

The problem of varieties was now manageable. Instead of dozens of vaccines, Salk would only have to find a way to grow and inactivate the three major strains of virus. The critical problem here was the necessity that in order to produce millions of doses of vaccine, one had to first have a means to grow the virus. Since the polio virus would only grow in primates, much research required the use of live monkeys.

Other scientists solved the problem. At the same time that Salk was perfecting his viral techniques with Thomas Francis, Jr., John Enders at Harvard was developing a method for growing the polio virus in laboratory cells. Salk availed himself of this technique, growing large quantities of the virus in monkey kidney cells in laboratory vessels.

Once Salk had his virus, he tested inactivation procedures using the chemical formalin. Carried out correctly, the procedure resulted in a vaccine composed of dead virus that could still immunize people effectively.

Although Salk's killed vaccine has been largely replaced by an attenuated form developed by Albert Sabin, its use in the 1950s and 1960s saved the lives of thousands of children. By the 1990s, poliomyelitis had been eradicated in the Western Hemisphere.

Bibliography

Polio and the Salk Vaccine. New York: Public Affairs Committee, 1955.

Blakeslee, Alton. *Polio and the Salk Vaccine: What You Should Know About It.* New York: Grosset & Dunlap, 1956.

Wilson, John. *Margin of Safety: The Story of Poliomyelitis Vaccine.* London: Collins, 1963.

The Process of Immunization

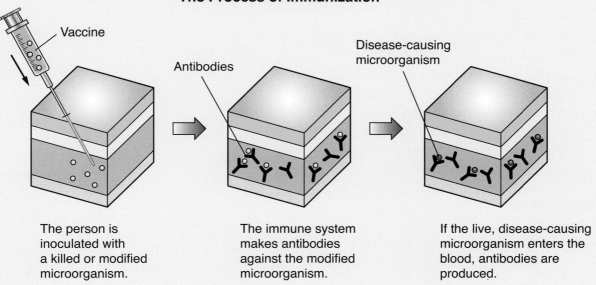

Vaccine

Antibodies

Disease-causing microorganism

The person is inoculated with a killed or modified microorganism.

The immune system makes antibodies against the modified microorganism.

If the live, disease-causing microorganism enters the blood, antibodies are produced.

A Hero to the Public

Salk became a household name. Among his honors were a Presidential Citation in 1955, a Congressional Gold Medal in 1955, the Albert Lasker Award in 1956, the Mellon Institute Award in 1969, and the Presidential Medal of Freedom in 1977. He received the Robert Koch Medal from Germany, while France named him a Chevalier de la Légion d'honneur. Although nominated, he was never named a Nobel laureate. His greatest reward was the knowledge of being instrumental in the eradication of a terrible disease.

In 1963, funded in part through the March of Dimes, the Salk Institute for Biological Studies was built in La Jolla, California, a suburb of San Diego. Salk became its first director.

The Salk Institute

Salk had long hoped for an institute where outstanding scientists could gather for research on topics important for humanity. The creation of the Salk Institute was the fulfillment of a lifetime dream. The institute, situated on land overlooking the Pacific Ocean, became a magnet for many important scientists.

During his later years, Salk carried out research on a variety of subjects, such as cancer and acquired immunodeficiency syndrome (AIDS). He also found more time to relax with his hobbies: poetry and painting. Weakened by congestive heart failure, Salk died on June 23, 1995.

Bibliography

By Salk

"A Simplified Procedure for Titrating Hemagglutinating Capacity of Influenza Virus and Corresponding Antibody," *Journal of Immunology*, 1944.

"Studies in Human Subjects on Active Immunization Against Poliomyelitis: 1. A Preliminary Report of Experiments in Progress," *Journal of the American Medical Association*, 1953.

"Considerations in the Preparation and Use of Poliomyelitis Virus Vaccine," *Journal of the American Medical Association*, 1955.

"Persistence of Immunity After Administration of Formalin-Treated Poliovirus Vaccine," *The Lancet*, 1960.

"A Review of Theoretical, Experimental, and Practical Considerations in the Use of Formaldehyde for the Inactivation of Poliovirus," *Annals of New York Academy of Sciences*, 1960 (with J. Gori).

Man Unfolding, 1972.

The Survival of the Wisest, 1973.

"Control of Influenza and Poliomyelitis with Killed Virus Vaccines," *Science*, 1977 (with Darrell Salk).

"Noninfectious Poliovirus Vaccine," *Vaccines*, 1988 (with Jacques Drucker; Stanley Plotkin and Edward Mortimer, Jr., eds.).

About Salk

Rowland, John. *The Polio Man: The Story of Dr. Jonas Salk*. New York: Roy, 1961.

Carter, Richard. *Breakthrough: The Saga of Jonas Salk*. New York: Trident Press, 1966.

Paul, John. *A History of Poliomyelitis*. New Haven, Conn.: Yale University Press, 1971.

(Richard Adler)

Lazzaro Spallanzani

Disciplines: Bacteriology, biology, earth science, and physiology

Contribution: Spallanzani helped discredit spontaneous generation, demonstrated the importance of semen in fertilization, and showed digestion to be primarily a process of chemical dissolution.

Jan. 12, 1729	Born in Modena, Duchy of Modena (now Italy)
1744	Attends a Jesuit seminary in Reggio Emilia
1754	Earns a Ph.D. from the University of Bologna
1755	Takes a teaching post at the College of Reggio Emilia
1757	Lecturer at the University of Reggio Emilia
1757	Ordained a priest
1763	Accepts a teaching position at Modena University
1768	Fellow of the Royal Society of London
1769	Professor of natural history at the University of Pavia and director of Pavia's Museum of Natural History
1776	Elected to the Berlin Academy of Sciences
1783	Founds a marine zoological laboratory at Porto Venere
1784	Turns down the chair of natural history at the University of Padua
1788	Studies Etna and Vesuvius
Feb. 11, 1799	Dies in Pavia, Cisalpine Republic (now Italy)

Early Life

Lazzaro Spallanzani (pronounced "spahl-lahn-TSAH-nee") was born in a small town in northern Modena (now Italy). At the age of fifteen, he enrolled in a Jesuit seminary in nearby Reggio Emilia, where he excelled academically.

In 1749 Spallanzani began taking courses at the University of Bologna, with the intention of becoming a lawyer, like his father. After three years, he abandoned the study of law to pursue other interests, such as natural philosophy and theology. In 1757 he was ordained a priest. From that point on, he was known as "the Abbé Spallanzani."

Reggio Emilia and Modena

After earning a Ph.D. in 1754, Spallanzani held teaching positions, first at Reggio Emilia and then at Modena University. While at Modena, he published *Saggio di osservazioni microscopiche relative al sistema della generazione dei Signori Needham e Buffon* (1765), in which he discredited the theory of spontaneous generation, which held that living organisms could arise from lifeless matter. Three years later, he published *Prodromo di un' opera da imprimersi sopra le riproduzioni animali* (1768; *An Essay upon Animal Reproductions*, 1769), which described his experiments on tissue regeneration.

Pavia

In 1769 Spallanzani accepted a post at the University of Pavia. At that time, the city of Pavia was part of Austria. The Austrian government not only made Spallanzani a professor of natural history but also appointed him director of Pavia's Museum of Natural History. Thanks to Spallanzani's tireless efforts, the museum became one of the jewels of the Austrian Empire.

Not long after arriving at Pavia, Spallanzani performed a number of experiments in which he observed for the first time the minute vascular connections between arteries and veins in warm-blooded animals. In 1776 he published a book on the nature of animals and vegetables that contained more experimental evidence against spontaneous generation. That same year, he was elected to the Berlin Academy of Sciences by arrangement of Frederick the Great, king of Prussia.

Spallanzani turned his attention to gastric digestion. In a series of fascinating experiments, some of which he performed on himself, he demonstrated that digestion is a process of chemical dissolution, rather than one of grinding, fermentation, or putrefaction.

His findings on digestion were published in *Dissertazioni di fisica animale e vegetabile* (1780; *Dissertations Relative to the Natural History of Animals and Vegetables*, 1784). This treatise also contains an important section on the role of semen in the process of fertilization.

Discrediting the Theory of Spontaneous Generation

Spallanzani showed that microorganisms will grow in broth only when it has been contaminated by contact with air.

In the late seventeenth century, the Italian physician Francesco Redi performed a number of experiments proving that flies are not generated spontaneously from rotting meat. In 1748, however, at the urging of the Comte de Buffon (Georges-Louis Leclerc), the microscopist John Needham published experiments on boiled meat and vegetable juices that seemed to indicate that microorganisms, such as bacteria, do indeed arise by spontaneous generation.

Spallanzani refuted Needham's findings by using glass flasks with very slender necks that could be quickly sealed with a flame. He discovered that if broth is heated vigorously for one hour and then hermetically sealed in a glass container, it will remain sterile indefinitely. If the seal is broken, however, so that the broth is exposed to air, microorganisms soon proliferate in great numbers. Spallanzani's experiments not only discredited the theory of spontaneous generation but also would prove of practical importance to the canning industry.

Despite Spallanzani's efforts, many scientists continued to believe in spontaneous generation until Louis Pasteur finally put the issue to rest nearly a century later. Pasteur was so inspired by Spallanzani's example that he hung a portrait of his scientific hero in his apartment.

Bibliography

De Kruif, Paul. *Microbe Hunters.* New York: Blue Ribbon Books, 1926.

Bulloch, William. *The History of Bacteriology.* London: Oxford University Press, 1960.

Hankins, Thomas L. *Science and the Enlightenment.* Cambridge, England: Cambridge University Press, 1985.

Final Years

In 1784 Spallanzani received an offer to move to the prestigious University of Padua. To retain him at Pavia, Emperor Joseph II increased Spallanzani's salary and allowed him to take an extended leave of absence so that he could travel to Constantinople. Spallanzani used this opportunity to accumulate new specimens for his museum of natural history.

With apparently little concern for the inherent dangers, Spallanzani journeyed to Sicily and southern Italy in 1788 in order to study the volcanoes Mount Etna and Mount Vesuvius at close range. His findings and courageous adventures are described in *Viaggi alle due Sicilie e in alcune parti dell'Appennino* (1792-1797; *Travels in the Two Sicilies, and Some Parts of the Apennines,* 1798).

Spallanzani died on February 11, 1799. Characteristically, his mind was on science until the end. In the posthumously published *Mémoires sur la respiration* (1803), he describes experiments, carried out in the 1790s, demonstrating that living tissues consume oxygen and release carbon dioxide.

Bibliography

By Spallanzani

Saggio di osservazioni microscopiche relative al sistema della generazione dei Signori Needham e Buffon, 1765.

Prodromo di un' opera da imprimersi sopra le riproduzioni animali, 1768 (*An Essay upon Animal Reproductions,* 1769).

De' fenomeni della circolazione, 1773 (*Experiments upon the Circulation of the Blood Throughout the Vascular System,* 1801).

Opusculi di fisica animale e vegetabile, 1776 (*Tracts on the Nature of Animals and Vegetables,* 1799).

Dissertazioni di fisica animale e vegetabile, 1780 (*Dissertations Relative to the Natural History of Animals and Vegetables,* 1784).

Viaggi alle due Sicilie e in alcune parti dell'Appennino, 1792-1797 (*Travels in the Two Sicilies, and Some Parts of the Apennines,* 1798).

Mémoires sur la respiration, 1803.

About Spallanzani

Massaglia, Aldo. "Lazzaro Spallanzani," *Medical Life* 32 (May 1925).

Foster, Michael. *Lectures on the History of Physiology During the Sixteenth, Seventeenth, and Eighteenth Centuries.* 1901. Reprint. New York: Dover, 1970.

(William Tammone)

Wendell Meredith Stanley

Disciplines: Cell biology and chemistry
Contribution: Stanley was the first person to isolate and characterize a virus, proving that it was a macromolecule.

Aug. 16, 1904	Born in Ridgeville, Indiana
1926	Graduated from Earlham College
1929	Earns a Ph.D. in chemistry from the University of Illinois
1930	Receives a National Research Council fellowship
1931	Joins the Rockefeller Institute for Medical Research
1935	Announces the isolation of tobacco mosaic virus (TMV)
1936	Disputes the discovery of nucleic acid in TMV
1941	Elected to the National Academy of Sciences
1943	Develops the first effective influenza vaccine
1946	Awarded the Nobel Prize in Chemistry
1948	Director of the Virus Laboratory at the University of California
1959	Writes a public television series on viruses
1960	Obtains the complete amino acid sequence of TMV protein
1961	Publishes *Viruses and the Nature of Life*
June 15, 1971	Dies in Salamanca, Spain

Early Life

Wendell Meredith Stanley grew up in a small Indiana town, serving as delivery boy, reporter, and typesetter for his parents' newspaper. In 1922 he entered Earlham College. He excelled in athletics, making the all-Indiana football team in his senior year.

After receiving a B.S. in chemistry, Stanley traveled to the University of Illinois to visit the athletic department, planning to become a football coach. He also visited the chemistry department and was so impressed that he registered for its graduate program instead.

Stanley received a Ph.D. in 1929. In the same year, he married another chemistry graduate, Marion Staples Jay.

Research to 1932

By 1929, Stanley had thirteen published papers. His investigations focused on the synthesis and structure of the constituents of chaulmoogric

The Nature of Viruses

Viruses are nucleoproteins with nucleic acid as their active agent.

In 1935 Stanley isolated and crystallized the tobacco mosaic virus (TMV) by chemically treating extracts of diseased plant juices. His tests indicated that the virus was a protein. In 1936 British scientists found his work inaccurate, because six percent of the virus was ribonucleic acid (RNA). Stanley argued that the RNA was not an integral part of the virus molecule, the protein alone being the viral agent.

The debate over the nature of the virus continued into the 1940s. Discoveries made in Stanley's Virus Laboratory vindicated the British scientists. A Stanley appointee, Heinz Fraenkel-Conrat, separated TMV into its protein and RNA parts in 1955. Examined with the electron microscope, the protein consisted of hollow cylinders and RNA in long, thin strands. Only the RNA displayed viral activity. In the intact nucleoprotein virus, the RNA was tucked inside the protein cylinders. The protein thus served as a protective shield for the fragile RNA strands.

Stanley demonstrated that a virus was a chemical molecule capable of being isolated and characterized by chemical methods. His achievement, modified with the recognition that nucleic acids played the central role in the virus molecule, opened and shaped research into the 1950s in the field of molecular biology.

Bibliography

Fraenkel-Conrat, Heinz. "The Genetic Code of a Virus," *Scientific American* 211 (October, 1964).

Kendrew, John S. *The Thread of Life.* Cambridge, Mass.: Harvard University Press, 1968.

Fraenkel-Conrat, Heinz, Paul Kimball, and Jay Levy. *Virology.* New York: Academic Press, 1988.

oil, then the most promising chemical agents for treating leprosy.

After a postdoctoral year in Germany, he joined the Rockefeller Institute in New York. His superiors found him so outstanding in research that they invited him in 1932 to become the research chemist at the institute's new department of plant pathology in Princeton, New Jersey.

The Princeton Years

For the rest of his career, Stanley investigated the chemistry of plant viruses. In 1932 the nature of viruses was unknown. Scientists debated whether they were minute organisms or chemical molecules. In 1935 Stanley disclosed that the tobacco mosaic virus was a giant protein molecule, then elaborated its physical and chemical properties. He received the 1946 Nobel Prize in Chemistry for his achievements.

World War II diverted his research to the development of an influenza (flu) vaccine under government contract. He produced a multistrain, inactive-virus vaccine. First used in a 1943 type A epidemic, it greatly reduced the incidence of influenza and became the first flu vaccine to be tested and proven effective.

The University of California

In 1948 Stanley became the director of the new Virus Laboratory at the University of California, Berkeley. He shaped it into the largest research center of its kind.

During the 1950s anticommunist crusade, the state of California imposed a loyalty oath to the United States on university faculty. Stanley led the resistance to the requirement, strongly defending those who refused to sign the oath and bringing the legal issues to the courts, where the oath was declared unconstitutional.

Stanley also became concerned about the communication of science to the public. He wrote a public television series on viruses in 1959 and a popular book, *Viruses and the Nature of Life* (1961).

In the 1960s he devoted himself to the relationship of viruses to cancer and helped win passage of the 1971 National Cancer Act, a program to combat cancer through research and education. His death in 1971 followed a heart attack while he was attending an international conference on viruses in Spain.

Bibliography

By Stanley

"Chemical Studies on the Virus of Tobacco Mosaic: VI. The Isolation from Diseased Turkish Tobacco Plants of a Crystalline Protein Possessing the Properties of Tobacco-Mosaic Virus," *Phytopathology*, 1936.

"The Reproduction of Virus Proteins," *The American Naturalist*, 1938.

"Chemical Properties of Viruses," *Scientific Monthly*, 1941.

Problems and Trends in Virus Research, 1947 (with Thomas Rivers and Wilbur A. Sawyer).

"The Isolation and Properties of Crystalline Tobacco Mosaic Virus," *Les Prix Nobel en 1947*, 1949.

The Viruses: Biochemical, Biological, and Biophysical Properties, 1959 (as ed., with F. M. Burnet).

About Stanley

Williams, Greer. *Virus Hunters*. New York: Alfred A. Knopf, 1959.

Edsall, John T. "Wendell Meredith Stanley," *American Philosophical Society Yearbook 1971*. Philadelphia, Pa.: American Philosophical Society, 1972.

Kay, Lily E. "W. M. Stanley's Crystallization of the Tobacco Mosaic Virus," *Isis* 77 (1986).

(*Albert B. Costa*)

Edward Lawrie Tatum

Disciplines: Bacteriology and cell biology

Contribution: With George Wells Beadle, Tatum pioneered the study of gene function through the use of biochemical mutations.

Dec. 14, 1909	Born in Boulder, Colorado
1931	Earns a B.A. in chemistry at the University of Wisconsin
1932	Receives an M.S. in microbiology from Wisconsin
1934	Earns a Ph.D. in biochemistry at Wisconsin
1936	Awarded a General Education Board Fellowship to study in Utrecht, the Netherlands
1937-1945	Works at Stanford University with George Wells Beadle
1944	Joins the staff of the Office of Scientific Research and Development to produce penicillin
1946	Professor of microbiology at Yale University
1946	Collaborates with geneticist Joshua Lederberg
1948-1956	Returns to Stanford as a professor of biology
1953	Receives the Remsen Award of the American Chemical Society
1956	Chair of biochemistry at Stanford
1957-1975	Professor at the Rockefeller Institute (later Rockefeller University) in New York City
1958	Awarded the Nobel Prize in Physiology or Medicine
Nov. 5, 1975	Dies in New York

Early Life

Edward Lawrie Tatum was the first surviving son of Arthur L. Tatum, a physician who held doctorates in pharmacology and physiology, and Mabel Webb. Edward's twin brother, Elwood, died shortly after birth. The family moved often but settled in Madison, Wisconsin, in 1925, where Edward's father was a professor of pharmacology at the University of Wisconsin.

Edward Tatum, benefiting from the intellectual climate of his family and the city in which he lived, earned his B.A. in chemistry in 1931. In quick succession, he earned an M.S. in microbiology in 1932 and a doctorate in biochemistry in 1934, both at the University of Wisconsin.

Tatum won a fellowship in 1936 that took his family to Utrecht in the Netherlands. Although Tatum thought that his research there lacked focus, he was exposed to methods and theories of microbial culture and nutrition.

The Neurospora Work

From 1937 to 1945 Tatum worked at Stanford University on problems relating to the nutritional requirements and cellular biochemistry of microorganisms. As a reflection of his lifelong interest in teaching, he also developed a biochemistry graduate curriculum, which was unprecedented at the time.

In the early 1940s Tatum collaborated with George Wells Beadle on the research that would later earn them the Nobel Prize in Physiology or Medicine. They determined the chemical processes involved in the genetic inheritance patterns of a species of bread mold of the genus *Neurospora*.

Sexual Reproduction in Bacteria

After a semester at Washington University in St. Louis, Tatum accepted a tenured position in the botany department of Yale University in 1945. At Yale, Tatum worked with a student named Joshua Lederberg. Through a series of experiments, Tatum and Lederberg determined that bacteria, like animals and plants, reproduce sexually. This discovery was important in demonstrating the continuity of life from microorganisms to higher plants and animals.

In 1958 Tatum shared one half of the Nobel Prize in Physiology or Medicine with Beadle for their work on *Neurospora*, which demonstrated that genes act by regulating chemical events within cells. The other half of the award went to Lederberg.

Ups and Downs

While Tatum's scientific career seemed to move from one important discovery to another, his personal life was less straightforward.

Tatum married a fellow student, June Alton, in 1934. They had two daughters and divorced in 1956. Within a year, Tatum married Viola Kantor, an employee of the March of Dimes, for which he served as a scientific adviser. They remained together until Viola's death in 1974. Tatum himself

One Gene, One Enzyme

Enzymes are the primary products of genes and the means by which genes control cellular processes.

Working with George Wells Beadle, Tatum investigated the mechanisms of gene action through mutated forms of the bread mold *Neurospora*. By exposing the mold colonies to X-rays, they increased dramatically the number of mutant forms.

Growing these mutants on different kinds of culture media, Tatum and Beadle were able to determine which gene had mutated. Thus, on a culture to which vitamin B6 had been added, they found that a mutant mold colony grew normally, although it grew poorly or died on other kinds of growth media. This result suggested that the gene responsible for making vitamin B6 had been affected by the mutation. It also suggested that a single gene controls a single enzyme.

They proved that this induced mutation behaved exactly like a natural mutation and that genes have a direct role in the production of enzymes and thus the control of cellular biochemistry.

The methods that Tatum and Beadle developed to analyze developmental and physiological processes are central to studies of cell development, physiology, and genetics, and are of great importance to biotechnology.

Bibliography

Williams, Bryan L. and Keith Wilson, eds. *A Biologist's Guide to Principles and Techniques of Practical Biochemistry*. New York: American Elsevier, 1975.

McGilvery, Robert W., ed. *Biochemistry: A Functional Approach*. Philadelphia, Pa.: W. B. Saunders, 1983.

Wilson, Keith and John M. Walker, eds. *Principles and Techniques of Practical Biochemistry*. 4th ed. Cambridge, England: Cambridge University Press, 1994.

suffered from poor health during his final years, and he died at his home in New York City in 1975.

Bibliography

By Tatum

"Experimental Control of Development and Differentiation," *American Naturalist*, 1941 (with George Wells Beadle).

"Genetic Control of Biochemical Reactions in *Neurospora*," *Proceedings of the National Academy of Sciences of the United States of America*, 1942 (with Beadle).

"The Genetic Control of Biochemical Reactions in *Neurospora*: A Mutant Strain Requiring Isoleucine and Valine," *Archives of Biochemistry*, 1943 (with David Bonner and Beadle).

"X-Ray Induced Growth Factor Requirements in Bacteria," *Proceedings of the National Academy of Sciences of the United States of America*, 1944 (with C. H. Gray).

"Novel Genotypes in Mixed Cultures of Biochemical Mutants of Bacteria," *Cold Spring Harbor Symposium on Quantitative Biology*, 1946 (with Joshua Lederberg).

"Gene Recombination in *Escherichia coli*," *Nature*, 1946 (with Lederberg).

About Tatum

Lederberg, Joshua. "Edward Lawrie Tatum," *Biographical Memoirs of the National Academy of Sciences of the United States of America* 59 (1990).

Wasson, Tyler, ed. "Tatum, Edward L.," *Nobel Prize Winners: An H. W. Wilson Biographical Dictionary*. New York: H. W. Wilson, 1987.

(*Christopher S. W. Koehler*)

Harold E. Varmus

Disciplines: Cell biology and virology

Contribution: Varmus won the Nobel Prize in Physiology or Medicine for discovering the genes that give rise to cancer.

Dec. 18, 1939	Born in Oceanside, Long Island, New York
1966	Earns an M.D. from Columbia University Medical School
1966-1968	Resident physician at Columbia-Presbyterian Hospital
1968	Joins Ira Pastan's laboratory at the National Institutes of Health (NIH)
1970	Joins J. Michael Bishop at the University of California, San Francisco (UCSF)
1970-1979	Ascends to the rank of professor
1982	Wins the Lasker Foundation Award
1984	Becomes American Cancer Society Research Professor of Molecular Virology at UCSF
1984	Elected to the National Academy of Sciences
1988	Elected to the American Academy of Arts and Sciences
1989	With Bishop, awarded the Nobel Prize in Physiology or Medicine
1988-1989	Works in the laboratory at the Whitehead Institute
1993-1999	Appointed director of the NIH
2000-2010	President of Memorial Sloan-Kettering Cancer Center
2009	Co-chair of Council of Advisors on Science and Technology
2010-present	Director of National Cancer Institute

Early Life

Harold Eliot Varmus was born to well-educated parents on Long Island just before World War II. His father was a physician, and his mother was a social worker. He attended public schools that, he later wrote, were "dominated by athletics and rarely inspiring intellectually." Originally planning to follow in his father's footsteps, he eventually turned to experimental science "dangerously late in a prolonged adolescence."

Entering Amherst College with the intention of fulfilling premedical requirements, Varmus became "devoted to Dickensian novels and anti-establishment journalism." He earned his B.A. in literature from Amherst and then indulged himself with "a year of Anglo-Saxon and metaphysical poetry at Harvard graduate school" before returning to his original goal. He earned a medical degree from Columbia and spent two years as a resident physician at Columbia-Presbyterian Hospital in New York City.

His ambitions turned toward a career in academic medicine, and he applied for research training at the National Institutes of Health (NIH). "Perhaps because his wife was a poet," Varmus later remarked, "Ira Pastan agreed to take me into his laboratory, despite my lack of scientific credentials."

His time at NIH led him to an interest in the viruses that cause cancer in animals. During the summer of 1969, Varmus "combined a backpacking vacation in California with a search for a suitable place to study tumor viruses." The search led him to join J. Michael Bishop's research team at the University of California, San Francisco (UCSF), the following summer. He remained at UCSF, reaching the rank of professor by 1979.

The Genetic Basis of Cancer

In 1970 two explanations for the genetic basis of cancer were being offered, and Varmus was determined to explore them. One was the "provirus" hypothesis of Howard Temin, which proposed that tumor viruses insert a copy of their genetic code into the deoxyribonucleic acid (DNA) of each cell that they invade. Before Varmus could make a start, however, the hypothesis was confirmed by Temin and David Baltimore.

The other hypothesis, which did not actually contradict the provirus theory, was the "virogene-oncogene" hypothesis. After five years of work, Bishop and Varmus confirmed part of this conjecture, but they also discovered a surprising

Oncogenes and Cancer

Cells contain proto-oncogenes, which normally control cell growth and development but which can cause cancer when they go awry.

In 1911 Peyton Rous discovered a virus that causes sarcoma, a type of cancer, in chickens. The Rous sarcoma virus (RSV) causes the cell that it infects and all of its descendants to reproduce uncontrollably—a phenomenon that reveals information about the origins of cancer.

The virogene-oncogene hypothesis explored by Varmus and J. Michael Bishop suggests that normal animal cells contain genes called oncogenes that, when activated, cause cells to become cancerous. These oncogenes are normally turned off, but they may be activated by chemicals or radiation. It is supposed that these oncogenes found their way into an animal's genome in ancient times from infection of an ancestor's egg by a virus carrying the corresponding virogene. New infection by a virus carrying an active virogene would also cause cancer.

Varmus and Bishop isolated the virogene in a small piece of the RSV genome and showed that a copy

of it was present in uninfected chicken cells—partially confirming the virogene-oncogene hypothesis. Further inspired experiments indicated that the gene, instead of originating in the virus, was actually a normal cellular gene that had been captured by an ancestor of the virus.

Varmus and Bishop collected more evidence showing this oncogene to be an important cellular gene that controls cell replication and development in most animals. By the late 1990s, more than seventy such proto-oncogenes were known to have roles in normal cell development.

Bibliography

Varmus, Harold and Robert A. Weinberg. *Genes and the Biology of Cancer.* New York: Scientific American Library, 1993.

Cavenee, W. K. and R. L. White. "The Genetic Basis of Cancer," *Scientific American* 272 (March, 1995).

Mendelsohn, John, et al. *The Molecular Basis of Cancer.* Philadelphia, Pa.: W. B. Saunders, 1995.

and important difference. Further work by the UCSF team and others proved the importance of their work, and, fourteen years later, they were awarded the Nobel Prize in Physiology or Medicine for their discoveries.

From Scientist to Administrator

By the late 1990s, Varmus had co-authored more than 300 scientific papers and served on several scientific advisory groups. He was chair of the committee that, in 1986, chose the name "human immunodeficiency virus" (HIV) for the virus that causes acquired immunodeficiency syndrome (AIDS).

In a significant departure from his scientific career, Varmus was selected by President Bill Clinton in 1993 to direct the NIH. Thus, Varmus returned to Bethesda, Maryland, to manage the institute where he began his research. Scientists often make poor managers, as his critics were quick to point out, but Varmus proved to be the exception—perhaps because of his broad interests in literature and outdoor recreation as well as in laboratory science.

Varmus then spent ten years as president of the Memorial Sloan-Kettering Cancer Center, growing its research and overseeing the creation of a cancer biology graduate program. In 2009 he was selected to serve as co-chair to President Obama's Council of Advisors on Science and Technology, and, in 2010, Varmus became the head of the National Cancer Institute.

Bibliography

By Varmus

"Integration of Deoxyribonucleic Acid Specific for Rous Sarcoma Virus After Infection of Permissive and Nonpermissive Hosts," *Proceedings of the National Academy of Sciences of the United States of America*, 1973. (with P. K. Vogt and J. Michael Bishop).

"DNA Related to the Transforming Gene(s) of Avian Sarcoma Viruses Is Present in Normal Avian DNA," *Nature*, 1976 (with D. Stehelin, Bishop, and Vogt).

"Form and Function of Retroviral Proviruses," *Science*, 1982.

"Oncogenes and Transcriptional Control," *Science*, 1987.

"Reverse Transcription," *Scientific American*, 1987.

"Polymerase Gene Products of Hepatitis B Viruses Are Required for Genomic RNA Packaging as Well as for Reverse Transcription," *Nature*, 1990 (with R. C. Hirsch, J. E. Lavine, L. J. Chang, and D. Ganem).

Genes and the Biology of Cancer, 1993 (with Robert A. Weinberg).

About Varmus

Fox, Daniel M., Marcia Meldrum, and Ira Rezak, eds. *Nobel Laureates in Medicine or Physiology: A Biographical Dictionary*. New York: Garland, 1990.

Magill, Frank N., ed. "Harold E. Varmus," *The Nobel Prize Winners: Physiology or Medicine*, Pasadena, Calif.: Salem Press, 1991.

Wasson, Tyler, ed. *Nobel Prize Winners: Supplement*. New York: H. W. Wilson, 1992.

"Harold Varmus to Step Down as President of Memorial Sloan-Kettering Cancer Center," Memorial Sloan-Kettering Cancer Center, January 12, 2010, http://www.mskcc.org/pressroom/press/harold-varmus-step-down-president-msk-center

"Director's Page," National Cancer Institute, http://www.cancer.gov/aboutnci/director/biography

(Randy Hudson)

Rudolf Virchow

Disciplines: Bacteriology, biology, cell biology, immunology, medicine, and physiology

Contribution: Virchow's work in pathology and cell histology established the field of cellular pathology, provided a deeper understanding of several diseases, and influenced public health and sanitation standards.

Oct. 13, 1821	Born in Schivelbein, Pomerania, Prussia (now Swidin, Poland)
1843	Earns a medical degree from the University of Berlin
1846	Joins the staff at Charité Hospital
1847	Lecturer at Berlin
1847	Helps establish the journal *Archiv für pathologische Anatomie und Physiologie und für klinische Medizin*
1848	Conducts a government study of a typhus epidemic in Silesia
1849	Professor at the University of Würzburg
1854	Publishes the first volume of *Handbuch der speziellen Pathologie und Therapie*
1856	Professor at the University of Berlin and head of its Institute of Pathology
1858	Publishes a classic work on cellular pathology
1861	Elected to the Prussian Diet (assembly) and forms the liberal party
1870	Begins work on anthropology, ethnology, and Darwinism
1901	His eightieth birthday is honored with a global festival
Sept. 5, 1902	Dies in Berlin, Germany

Early Life

From an early age, Rudolf Ludwig Karl Virchow (pronounced "FIHR-khoh") developed a sense of skepticism: he questioned unbridled hypothesis formation and inexact reasoning cloaked as science. He would maintain this analytic acuity and critical vigor over a fifty-year career.

Virchow's exposure to medicine began with a military fellowship at the Friedrich-Wilhelms Institute. In 1843, after earning a medical degree at the University of Berlin, he gave a prestigious presentation on phlebitis that corrected common misconceptions. A series of lectures on pathology followed, and his fame grew rapidly. In 1847 he cofounded the journal *Archiv für pathologische Anatomie und Physiologie und für klinische Medizin.*

Virchow believed that medicine should influence culture and political processes. In an 1848 report, he criticized the Prussian government as the cause of a typhus epidemic in Silesia; his recommendation was political autonomy. Although Virchow excelled at statesmanship, notably public health issues, his liberalism, scientific insight, and public health reform efforts created many enemies. His position at Charité Hospital in Berlin was suspended in 1849, and his progressive journal, *Medizinische Reform*, ended that same year.

Concentrating on Pathology

When his position at Charité Hospital was jeopardized, Virchow accepted a professorship at the University of Würzburg, which was located in Bavaria, so freeing him of Prussian persecution. He devoted his efforts toward cellular pathology and began publishing *Handbuch der speziellen Pathologie und Therapie*, a six-volume foundational masterpiece on scientific pathology.

Returning to Berlin in 1856, Virchow continued research as a professor at the University of Berlin, directing its Institute of Pathology. He presented a series of twenty lectures, with demonstrations of cellular pathology, which influenced the discipline significantly. In 1858 he published these lectures, with numerous engravings, in the first edition of *Die Cellularpathologie* (*Cellular Pathology*, 1860), a fundamental text that would be translated into many languages. Virchow worked on a second revised edition while preparing *Die krankhaften Geschwülste* (1863-1867)—a treatise covering tumors.

A Return to Politics

With his renown came a revitalized interest in political reform. Virchow's efforts in municipal politics led to the establishment of sewage and water improvement projects in Berlin. He avidly served as a founder of the liberal party and a top representative, and made quite an impact in the political sphere, coming close to a personal duel with statesman Otto von Bismarck.

While debating against Germanic militarism and consolidation, Virchow helped mobilize and

Cellular Foundations of Pathology

Virchow's greatest contribution to science was the principle that cells arise from other cells, which complements and extends Louis Pasteur's organic continuity principle.

Virchow carefully formulated the cellular-based and organ-based models of pathology. Disease and inflammation were given a reasoned and localized causality, overturning popular pseudoscientific misconceptions. He opposed the humoral view, which based health completely on the state of a fundamental living fluid—called "lymph," "cytoblastema," "plasma," and other names—carried by the bloodstream. Many of these terms have valid but different meanings in modern biology. He likewise opposed the neural pathologist school, which made the nervous system the primary determining factor. Virchow refined Theodor Schwann's cell theory and its variants, most notably removing the concept of cell generation from noncellular forms.

Virchow identified, named, and studied leukemia, thrombosis, and embolism. Among the structures that he discovered were fibrinogen, amyloid (and its degeneration), hematoidin, and myelin. His extensive research included inflammation and tumor development, focusing on their physiological mechanisms.

Bibliography

King, Lester S. *Growth of Medical Thought*. Chicago, Ill.: University of Chicago Press, 1974.

Rubin, Emanuel and John L. Farber. *Pathology*. 2d ed. Philadelphia, Pa.: J. B. Lippincott, 1994.

Cotran, Ramzi S., Vinay Kumar, and Stanley L. Robbins. *Robbins Pathologic Basis of Disease*. 5th ed. Philadelphia, Pa.: W. B. Saunders, 1994.

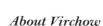

establish medical support for the casualties of the Franco-Prussian War. He wanted medicine to have a key and benevolent role in the political destiny of nations.

Other Studies

In the field of anthropology, Virchow created a German professional society. He conducted research with Heinrich Schliemann at the site of ancient Troy and wrote a monograph on artifacts in Trojan graves.

In ethnology, he directed surveys of German schoolchildren and found significant diversity. He worked against unscientific ethnological presuppositions and debated against the misapplication of evolution theory to metaphysics by E. H. Haeckel, his former student.

Virchow's work in public health and epidemiology is also recognized. He knew that lack of sanitation, governmental neglect, and political conditions cause diseases such as trichinosis and typhus, and he saw the need for public health care.

In 1901 Virchow's eightieth birthday was celebrated with a global festival. He died in Berlin almost a year later.

Bibliography

By Virchow

Handbuch der speziellen Pathologie und Therapie, 1854–1876 (6 vols.).

Die Cellularpathologie, in ihrer Begründung auf physiologische und pathologische Gewebelehre, 1858 (*Cellular Pathology, as Based upon Physiological and Pathological Histology*, 1860).

Die krankhaften Geschwülste, 1863–1867 (3 vols.).

Gesammelte Abhandlungen aus dem Gebiete der öffentlichen Medicin und der Seuchenlehre, 1879 (*Collected Essays on Public Health and Epidemiology*, 1985).

Virchow Bibliographie, 1843–1901, 1901.

Disease, Life, and Man: Selected Essays by Rudolf Virchow, 1958.

About Virchow

Ackerknecht, Erwin H. *Rudolf Virchow: Doctor, Statesman, Anthropologist*. Madison, Wis.: University of Wisconsin Press, 1953.

Pridan, D. "Rudolf Virchow and Social Medicine in Historical Perspective," *Medical History* 8 (1964).

Rather, L. J. *A Commentary on the Medical Writings of Rudolf Virchow*. San Francisco, Calif.: Norman, 1991.

(John Panos Najarian)

Selman Abraham Waksman

Disciplines: Bacteriology and biology

Contribution: Waksman was awarded the Nobel Prize in Physiology or Medicine for his discovery of streptomycin, the first antibiotic effective against tuberculosis.

July 22, 1888	Born in Novaya Priluka, Russian Empire (now Priluki, Ukraine)
1910	Emigrates to the United States
1918	Earns a Ph.D. in biochemistry at the University of California, Berkeley
1927	Publishes a seminal text entitled *Principles of Soil Microbiology*
1929	Professor of soil microbiology at Rutgers University
1930-1942	Director of the marine microbiology division of the Woods Hole Marine Biological Laboratory
1939	Elected to the National Academy of Sciences
1944	Isolates and characterizes streptomycin
1948	Receives the Albert and Mary Lasker Award
1950	Made a Commander of the French Legion of Honor
1952	Awarded the Nobel Prize in Physiology or Medicine for his discovery of streptomycin
Aug. 16, 1973	Dies in Hyannis, Massachusetts

Early Life

Selman Abraham Waksman was born and spent his early youth in Novaya Priluka, a small Jewish town in the Kiev region of the Ukraine. He grew up in a household run by his grandmother, mother, and seven aunts, and attended a government Latin school in nearby Zhitomir and later in Odessa.

In 1910, after finishing his schooling, Waksman emigrated to the United States. He lived with relatives in New Jersey and attended Rutgers University. At Rutgers, Waksman studied under Jacob G. Lipman, a bacteriologist and dean of the college of agriculture, who was also an immigrant from the Ukraine. Waksman was particularly interested in the biochemistry and microbiology of soil, and completed an M.A. in 1916. He returned to Rutgers in 1919 after earning his Ph.D. in biochemistry at the University of California, Berkeley. Waksman remained at Rutgers for his entire career, distinguishing himself as one of the nation's foremost soil biologists.

Streptomycin

An antibiotic isolated from the soil microbe Streptomyces griseus, Streptomycin was the first drug used successfully to fight tuberculosis and numerous other bacterial diseases.

Waksman spent his career studying soil microbes. As an undergraduate, he used a microscope to examine colonies of fungi and bacteria in soil samples. He found minute colonies of microbes that were neither fungi nor bacteria; he later learned that these microbes belonged to a relatively obscure group known as actinomycetes.

Waksman was amazed at the large number of microorganisms in the soil and became convinced that they did not live in distinct groups but rather that they comprised a complex group of interrelationships. He derived two principles from his early soil studies: that soil is made up of a large number of different groups of microorganisms, each possessing different functions and activities, and that these microorganisms influence one another in a variety of ways.

Waksman's desire to learn more about the role of actinomycetes in soil processes led him to pursue a doctorate in biochemistry. By 1936, he was able to demonstrate that actinomycetes exert considerable influence over the activities of fungi and bacteria in the soil. His decision to seek disease-fighting substances from actinomycetes began in 1939, when his former student René Dubos isolated tyrocidine, a product of soil bacilli that had a destructive effect on disease-producing bacteria. He was also inspired by the need to develop new drugs to treat casualties from World War II.

With financial support from Merck & Co in Rahway, New Jersey, Waksman developed and applied screening techniques for isolating antibiotics in soil and other samples. Over the next ten years, he and his co-workers isolated ten antibiotics from actinomycetes, including three with significant clinical applications: actinomycin, streptomycin, and neomycin.

Streptomycin is second only to penicillin in its effectiveness as a broad-spectrum antibiotic. The antibiotic acts by interfering with a microorganism's ability to synthesize certain vital proteins. Streptomycin was the first antibiotic effective against gram-negative bacteria. Susceptible microbes included those responsible for tuberculosis, plague, influenza, spinal meningitis, typhoid fever, and urinary tract infections. Clinical effectiveness against tuberculosis was demonstrated in 1944, and the drug was mass-produced and distributed worldwide by the late 1940s.

Because treatment of bacteria with streptomycin increases the chance of changes in the hereditary material of cells, however, many bacteria are now resistant to streptomycin. As a result, physicians are encountering increasing cases of antibiotic-resistant bacteria. For example, by the 1990s, tuberculosis was experiencing a resurgence among homeless people in the United States.

Bibliography

Waksman, Selman A. and H. A. Lechevalier. *Actinomycetes and Their Antibiotics,* Baltimore, Md.: Williams & Wilkins, 1953.

Waksman, Selman A. *The Antibiotic Era: A History of the Antibiotics and of Their Role in the Conquest of Infectious Diseases and in Other Fields of Human Endeavor.* Tokyo: Waksman Foundation of Japan, 1975.

Streptomycin and the "White Plague"

In 1944 Waksman and his colleagues isolated streptomycin, a new antibiotic taken from actinomycetes found growing in the throats of chickens. In 1945 clinical trials of streptomycin in the treatment of human tuberculosis were an enormous success. The ability of the drug to attack the gramnegative tubercle bacillus meant that humankind finally had an effective cure for the disease that had been called "consumption" and "the white plague."

Waksman's achievement was followed by many awards, culminating with the 1952 Nobel Prize in Physiology or Medicine. In his 1954 autobiography, he noted that, since 1940, when the term "antibiotics" did not even exist, the new "wonder drugs" had brought about a medical revolution. He believed that antibiotics could control all infectious diseases of humans and animals. By 1965, more than 25,000 different antibiotic products were saving the lives of millions of patients who would otherwise have fallen prey to diseases caused by bacteria. Waksman died in 1973 at the age of eighty-five.

Bibliography

By Waksman

Enzymes, 1926 (with Wilburt Davidson).

Principles of Soil Microbiology, 1927.

The Soil and the Microbe, 1931 (with Robert Starkey).

Humus, 1936.

Microbial Antagonisms and Antibiotic Substances, 1945.

The Literature on Streptomycin, 1948-1952.

Streptomycin, Its Nature, and Practical Application, 1949.

The Actinomycetes, 1950-1966.

Soil Microbiology, 1952.

Actinomycetes and Their Antibiotics, 1953 (with Hubert Lechevalier).

Sergei N. Winogradsky, 1953.

My Life with the Microbes, 1954.

Perspectives and Horizons in Microbiology: A Symposium, 1955.

The Conquest of Tuberculosis, 1964.

Jacob O. Lipman, 1966.

Actinomycin, 1968.

The Antibiotic Era: A History of the Antibiotics and of Their Role in the Conquest of Infectious Diseases and in Other Fields of Human Endeavor, 1975.

About Waksman

Woodruff, H. Boyd, ed. *Scientific Contributions of Selman A. Waksman: Selected Articles Published in Honor of His Eightieth Birthday, July 22, 1968.* New Brunswick, N.J.: Rutgers University Press, 1968.

Magill, Frank N., ed. "Selman Abraham Waksman," *The Nobel Prize Winners: Physiology or Medicine*, Pasadena, Calif.: Salem Press, 1991.

(Peter Neushul)

Harald zur Hausen

Discipline: Virology

Contribution: Known for discovering the link between human papillomavirus (HPV), which causes genital warts, and cervical cancer

March 11, 1936	Born in in Gelsenkirchen, Germany
1960	Earned an M.D. from the University of Düsseldorf
1961	First research job at the Institute of Microbiology in Düsseldorf
1966	Postdoctoral fellowship at the Children's Hospital of Philadelphia
1968	Appointment at the University of Würzburg, Germany
1972	Appointed chair of the Institute of Clinica and begins work with human papillomaviruses (HPV)
1983	Isolates HPV-16 DNA and identifies it in fifty percent of cervical cancer biopsies
1986	Receives the Charles Mott Prize
1993	President of the Organization of the European Cancer Institutes
1996	Receives the Ernst-Jung Prize for Medicine
1999	Receives the Charles Rodolphe Brupbacher Prize for Cancer Research
2008	Awarded the Nobel Prize in Physiology or Medicine for his work linking HPV with the development of cervical cancer.
2009	Member of the National Academy of Sciences

Early Life

Harald zur Hausen was born as the youngest of four children in 1936 in Gelsenkirchen, Germany, and spent his childhood in this heavily bombed area during World War II. The bombing raids in 1943 closed schools, leaving some gaps in his education. Zur Hausen eventually overcame this interrupted education, though he was not the top student in his class. His parents moved to northern Germany in 1950, and he completed high school in 1955.

Zur Hausen knew even as a child that he wanted to be a scientist. He took great pleasure in learning about birds, flowers, and biology in general. When the time came for zur Hausen to go to college, he contemplated studying his first love, biology. However, upon acceptance to the University of Bonn, he decided to pursue medicine. His confidence in his talent for science grew after he passed his first exam and first five semesters with high marks. His schooling was particularly challenging because while studying medicine he also opted to take biology courses. He then spent one year at the University of Hamburg and the Medical Academy in Düsseldorf (now the University of Düsseldorf), graduating from there in 1960.

Physician and Researcher

Zur Hausen's love of science persisted. He was determined to continue in the field, yet he also wanted to be a licensed medical practitioner. He therefore spent two years in a medical internship, which exposed him to surgery, internal medicine, and finally gynaecology and obstetrics. It was these last two subjects that proved to be the most engaging for him.

Zur Hausen knew that what he really wanted to do was research and began his first job at the Institute of Microbiology in Düsseldorf. He was fascinated by infectious diseases and spent more than three years there trying to induce a cowpox virus. Resources, though, were limited. He had to teach himself how to do lab work and did not receive much guidance or help with his research. Frustrated by his own limitations and the lack of cooperation, he decided to leave and sought a postdoctoral position in the United States. Accepting an offer from the Division of Virology at the Children's Hospital of Philadelphia, zur Hausen, his wife and young son moved to the United States in 1966.

HPV Virus and Cervical Cancer

HPV is the leading cause of cervical cancer, the second most common cancer among women.

In the early 1970s zur Hausen set up a program to investigate the possible causes for skin warts. He plunged into research, knowing that the DNA of viruses could be detected by searches for viral DNA, as it exists in a nonproductive state in tumors. In the early research stages, zur Hausen's team extracted papilloma DNA from a wart found on the foot, or plantar wart, but were discouraged to find that this DNA did not react with genital warts. This experiment and negative results in cervical cancer and genital warts biopsies hinted that there were probably different types of papilloma viruses.

Zur Hausen believed that there was a strong relationship between viruses and cancer. In 1979 two of zur Hausen's co-workers, Lutz Gissman and Ethel-Michele de Villiers isolated and cloned the first genital wart DNA, HPV-6. Though not detected in cervical cancer biopsies, it was useful in isolating a closely related papilloma virus, HPV-11. Using this as a probe, they discovered that one out of every twenty-four cervical cancer biopsies was positive. In 1983 and 1984 they were able to isolate HPV-16 and HPV-18 respectively, with HPV-16 present in fifty percent of cervical cancer biopsies, and HPV-18 in slightly more than twenty percent. From this research, they determined that the viruses played a key role in the development of cervical cancer.

When the results were first presented, they were met with silence and general indifference, as many were skeptical about the theory of viruses causing cancer. But the results soon began to be accepted in scientific communities. The discovery led to a better understanding of the link between papilloma viruses and cervical cancer and eventually to a preventive vaccine.

Bibliography

McIntyre, Peter. "Finding the viral link: the story of Harald zur Hausen", *Cancer World*, http://www.cancerworld.org/Articles/Issues/7/July-August-2005/Masterpiece/141/Finding-the-viral-linkthe-story-ofHarald-zur-Hausen.html

Studying the Links Between Some Viruses and Cancers

In 1968 Eberhard Wecker, head of the new Institute for Virology at the University of Würzberg, offered zur Hausen an independent research group and support for a start in the German academic system. He accepted the offer and moved back to Germany with his family in March, 1969. Exposed to research with the Epstein-Barr virus (EBV) while in Philadelphia, he decided to make this his primary area of focus, intending to demonstrate that EBV DNA is present in tumor cells in Burkitt's lymphoma, and does not produce a persistent infection, as assumed by many of his colleagues. His work eventually demonstrated that viruses exist in tumor DNA in human malignancies, or cancerous cells, and that these viruses can encourage tumor growth.

Appointed chair of the newly established Institute of Clinical Virology in Erlangen-Nürnberg, he changed his research agenda to focus on cervical cancer. The disease had been associated with an infectious agent, identified as herpes simplex type 2 (HSV-2) in the late 1960s. However, he and a colleague employed the same technique they used to identify EBV DNA in specific cancers to locate HSV-2. Finding no traces of the virus, zur Hausen began to explore another theory.

He had previously studied reports describing malignant conversion of genital warts into squamous cell carcinomas. He thought that perhaps the human papillomavirus, or HPV, which was known to cause genital warts, might be the cause of cervical cancer. His research showed that many different types of HPV existed, but that only a few types were responsible for causing cervical cancer. The major breakthrough in zur Hausen's research was the isolation of HPV types 16 and 18, which are two of the common types of HPV that cause cervical cancer among women.

Zur Hausen's work garnered him the Nobel Prize in Physiology or Medicine in 2008, which he shared with Françoise Barré-Sinoussi and Luc Montagnier for their discovery of HIV.

Bibliography

By zur Hausen

Infections Causing Human Cancer, 2007.
TT Viruses: The Still Elusive Human Pathogens, 2011 (ed. with Ethel-Michel de Villiers).

About zur Hausen

"Harald zur Hausen—Biographical," Nobelprize. org, http:// www.nobelprize.org/nobel_prizes/ medicine/laureates/2008/hausen-bio.html

"Prof. Dr. Harald zur Hausen Awarded Nobel Prize for Medicine," October 6, 2008, http:// www.uni-heidelberg.de/presse/news08/ press601e.html

Glossary

Amino acid: Any organic molecule containing at least one amine and one carboxyl (COOH) group. Amino acids are bound together in chains to form proteins.

Antibiotic: Any substance that destroys or inhibits the growth of microorganisms, especially bacteria.

Antibody: A substance, produced by an organism in reaction to the presence of foreign material, which inhibits the toxic effects of that material.

Antigen: A molecule capable of stimulating the production of antibodies by an organism.

Antiseptic: A substance that can kill disease-producing microorganisms.

Bacillus (pl. bacilli): One of a variety of rod-shaped bacteria.

Bacteriophage: One of a number of viruses that infect bacteria, causing their disintegration.

Cancer: One of a class of diseases characterized by abnormal cell growth that invades adjacent cell groups.

Capillary: The smallest blood-carrying vessel. Capillaries connect arteries and veins.

Cell: The smallest structural unit of a living organism capable of independent function.

Chromosome: The threadlike structures, composed primarily of DNA, which contain most of the genetic information of a cell.

Circulation: The movement of the blood through the system of arteries, veins, and capillaries as a result of the pumping of the heart.

Culture: The association of organisms under controlled conditions or the production of such an association (for example, the growth of bacteria for study).

Decay: The decomposition of organic matter resulting from the action of microorganisms.

Disease: An abnormal condition of an organism which causes impaired functioning.

DNA (deoxyribonucleic acid): The self-replicating molecule that is the fundamental carrier of hereditary material. Its structure is a double helix—a twisted ladder with sugars and phosphates forming the sides, and base pairs in the center forming the rungs.

Environment: The totality of external conditions that affect an organism or part of an organism.

Enzyme: A protein with chemical groups on its surface that allow it to be a catalyst for a chemical reaction.

Epidemic: A rapid and extensive spread of a contagious disease among a population.

Ether: In medicine, a volatile liquid widely used as an anesthetic.

Etiology: The cause or origin of something, such as a disease.

Fermentation: The enzyme-induced breakdown of large molecules (such as sugar) without the presence of oxygen, in order to extract energy.

Fertilization: The union of a sperm with an egg.

Fungus (pl. fungi, adj. fungal): A plantlike organism that does not produce its own food through photosynthesis, instead absorbing complex carbon compounds from other living or dead organisms. Fungal infections range from minor skin diseases to serious diseases of the lungs and other organs.

Gene: A portion of a DNA molecule that controls a hereditary characteristic of an organism, either individually or in combination with other genes.

Genome: All the genes contained in a single complete set of chromosomes.

Heredity: The transmission of characteristics from ancestor to descendant through genes.

Humors, theory of: The former theory that health is produced by an appropriate balance of four substances, or humors, in the body—blood, phlegm, yellow bile, and black bile.

Immune system: An organism's system for responding to foreign materials and microorganisms through the production of antibodies.

Immunity: The resistance of an organism to a disease.

Immunology: The medical field that studies the immune system and its functioning.

Inoculation: The process of introducing antigens into an organism, usually for the purpose of producing antibodies and therefore immunity.

Lysis: The bursting of a cell.

Metabolism: The sum total of chemical reactions that occur in an organism, or a subset of those reactions pertaining to a defined function.

Molecule: A stable group of atoms held together by chemical forces and entering into characteristic chemical reactions.

Oncogene: A gene that specifies the structure of an enzyme that is a catalyst for cancer-inducing events.

Pathogen: An organism that causes disease.

Polymer: A long chain of identical chemical units that are linked to form a single large molecule.

Progeny: The offspring or descendants of an organism.

Retrovirus: A family of RNA viruses which contain an enzyme that catalyzes the production of DNA and which integrate themselves into the host's chromosomes.

RNA (ribonucleic acid): One of a class of nucleic acids containing the sugar ribose which are involved in the transcription and translation of the genetic material in DNA.

Serum: The liquid portion of the blood from which all clotting elements have been removed.

Spontaneous generation: The regular spontaneous emergence of life out of inorganic materials, which was long assumed to be possible.

Transplantation: The removal of an organism or part of an organism from one environment and its introduction into another. This is often used to describe the removal of an organ or tissue from a donor to replace the defective organ or tissue of a recipient.

Ultraviolet light: Electromagnetic radiation with wavelengths just below those of the visible spectrum.

Vaccination: The injection of a virus, a bacterium, or their proteins (usually in a weakened form) into a body with the purpose of producing immunity.

Vector: In biology, an agent that carries an entity to a place where it can act; for example, ticks are vectors for the bacteria that produce Lyme disease in humans.

Virus: Any of a class of ultramicroscopic organisms containing nucleic acid and at least one protein. Viruses, which can reproduce only in living cells, often cause disease.

Vitamin: One of a class of organic compounds that an organism needs in small amounts but which it cannot synthesize for itself.

X-rays: Penetrating electromagnetic radiation produced by the collision of high-velocity electrons with a target. Also called Röntgen rays for Wilhelm Conrad Röntgen, who discovered them.